praise for
the power of you

"*The Power of You* is fresh air for the spirit: a real, practical pointer in the direction of the presence inside us all that, once met, changes everything for the oh-so-much better."

—VICTORIA MORAN, author of
Creating a Charmed Life and *Main Street Vegan*

"Dr. Chris Michaels is one of the finest spiritual teachers I know. *The Power of You* is a magnificent bridge into the glory and vast potential of the true You, your Higher Self. As you read, you'll find yourself moving out of the collective trance states of self-doubt, self-denial, and self-pity and that pervasive sense of inadequacy. Dr. Chris assists you in reclaiming your magnificence as you stand in the Light of Divine Love. Read this wonderful book, share it widely, and bring us all the gifts of your 'imprisoned splendor'!"

—DR. ROGER W. TEEL, Senior Minister and
Spiritual Director, Mile Hi Church, Denver

"God broke the mold after He created Chris Michaels. In *The Power of You*, Chris's brilliance and originality as a master teacher shine through on every page with authenticity, transparency, wit, wisdom, and a plethora of sidesplitting humor. If you are wise enough to follow his lead, Chris will guide you, prod you, lift you, but, mostly, inspire you to take full ownership of the power you were given to be yourself. The truth is that God broke the mold after He created *you* as well. Now is the time to prove it."

—DENNIS MERRITT JONES, award-winning author of
The Art of Uncertainty and *The Art of Being*

"Chris Michaels is the Norman Vincent Peale for our generation. He has written a 'gateway' book—one that introduces big, essential life questions about who we are and what we are here to do, and then answers them simply and clearly. You're going to read this book with a highlighter!"

—AUGUST GOLD, coauthor of
The Prayer Chest and *Multiply Your Blessings*

"Dr. Chris Michaels has written a passionate and compelling book about such questions as 'Why am I here?' and 'What am I supposed to be doing?' In bold, confident, and fearless language, he takes on the big ideas: God, your mind, and the very purpose of existence. At the end of the book I felt as if I had been picked up, dusted off, straightened out, and placed gently back on the path of my own soul's assignment."

—EDWARD VILJOEN, author of *The Power of Meditation*

"In *The Power of You*, Chris Michaels creates a portal into a vast new understanding of life. The ideas and images he projects are clear and palatable, even when addressing concepts that may otherwise seem elusive. *The Power of You* does not talk to us, but rather awakens a knowing within us that has been waiting patiently to emerge. This wonderful book will leave us all feeling better about ourselves and more open to exploring life's greatest mysteries."

—JOHN B. WATERHOUSE, President, Centers for Spiritual Living, and author of *Five Steps to Freedom*

"Discover yourself—in all your messy, powerful, human spiritual glory! With straight talk and deep wisdom, Chris Michaels leads you through key moments of self-awareness and personal growth. His explorations—ranging from our myth of God through your own story to the Power of the Mind and Word—reveal where we've been while beckoning us on to a more meaningful experience of ourselves and our lives. *The Power of You* is a great road map on how to get to live the life of your dreams."

—PETRA WELDES, Senior Minister, Center for Spiritual Living, Dallas

the

Power

of

You

JEREMY P. TARCHER/PENGUIN
A member of Penguin Group (USA) ▪ New York

the

Power

of

You

HOW TO LIVE YOUR
AUTHENTIC, EXCITING,
JOY-FILLED LIFE NOW!

Chris Michaels

JEREMY P. TARCHER/PENGUIN
Published by the Penguin Group
Penguin Group (USA) LLC
375 Hudson Street
New York, New York 10014

USA · Canada · UK · Ireland · Australia
New Zealand · India · South Africa · China

penguin.com.
A Penguin Random House Company

Most Tarcher/Penguin books are available at special quantity discounts for bulk purchase for sales promotions, premiums, fund-raising, and educational needs. Special books or book excerpts also can be created to fit specific needs. For details, write: Special.Markets@us.penguingroup.com.

Library of Congress Cataloging-in-Publication Data

Michaels, Chris, date.
  The power of you : how to live your authentic, exciting, joy-filled life now! / Chris Michaels.
    p.   cm.
  ISBN 978-0-399-16260-2
  1. Spirituality.   2. Self-acceptance.   3. Self-actualization
(Psychology)—Religious aspects.   I. Title.
  BL624.M473   2014   2013035202
  158.1—dc23

Printed in the United States of America
10 9 8 7 6 5 4 3 2 1

BOOK DESIGN BY EMILY S. HERRICK

While the author has made every effort to provide accurate telephone numbers, Internet addresses, and other contact information at the time of publication, neither the publisher nor the author assumes any responsibility for errors, or for changes that occur after publication. Further, the publisher does not have any control over and does not assume any responsibility for author or third-party websites or their content.

contents

Acknowledgments   *xi*

Introduction   *xiii*

one
A Bigger Universe—a Greater God   *1*

two
Self-Discovery   *33*

three
Self-Acceptance   *73*

four

Your Mind and How to Use It   *121*

five

Your Soul's Assignment   *171*

six

Self-Command   *202*

seven

The Final Frontier   *234*

Afterword   *261*

Appendix   *263*

I dedicate this book to seekers of truth,
to those left unsatisfied with what
has already been said or done in the world.

It was intended for people searching for
answers to the big questions in life such as:
What is the purpose of life? Why am I here?
What am I supposed to be doing?

acknowledgments

Writing a book is a labor of love. The words don't always come easy to the page. They have been brought here only after years of study, support and encouragement. We do not succeed in any endeavor merely by our own talents. We arrive at our success by standing on the shoulders of giants. Here is a brief list of some of the giants in my life:

The support and love of my partner, Aubrey Williams, over the last two decades has given me the courage and confidence to follow my dreams. I wish to thank my good friend Edward Viljoen, a man whom I've learned more from than just about anyone in the world.

Many thanks to my good friends Daniele Michaels, Robert Stovall, Jan McAdams, Wayne Gibson, Susan Phipps, Doug Greenbaum, John Tambasco and Kent McIntyre, who've always encouraged me to be myself and speak my truth, even when others couldn't understand. I wish to thank the staff and Core Council at Center for Spiritual Living in Kansas City. Without your support, I never would have been able to complete this project. And of course much praise to my publisher, Joel Fotinos, a brave soul and generous man. Thanks for your guidance and faith.

I leave my last recognition and gratitude to Spirit—that Presence and Power sustaining the universe, alive and conscious within its own creation. A power and wisdom is rising up within humanity, guiding us toward its own end. I am but one voice in a chorus of millions who have begun to trust that what is deep within them is holy and sacred. This is our time. We are the right people. We have everything we need to transform the world.

introduction

*We are like flies crawling across the ceiling of
the Sistine Chapel. We cannot see what angels and
gods lie underneath the threshold of our perceptions.*

—WILLIAM IRWIN THOMPSON,
Evil and World Order

I f you talk to professional actors or vocalists, many will
say when they're at their peak performance level they feel
a sense of some *other presence* on stage with them, something beyond themselves. It's as if a part of them is caught
up in the performance itself, and yet another part is watching it from a distance. That *other presence* seems bigger than
their own talent or personality. It is using their vocal cords
to sing or their personality to act. It is the higher self or

Spirit, expressing through them, the master artist expressing itself through their skill. It is the giver of the talent, the designer of the vocal cords.

Most artists sign their work. In the corner of a painting or underneath a sculpture is the signature of the genius who created it. That signature has been left on you as well by your Creator. You are a signed original, a masterpiece created by the universe's only Genius. Its imprint has been stamped on your heart. Its genius is alive inside your soul.

You are more than you think. You have more talent than you have yet expressed. You have more in you than you've let out. Like the flies crawling across the ceiling of the Sistine Chapel, you have been walking through life completely unaware of the power that resides within you.

In Oscar Wilde's play *Lady Windermere's Fan*, the characters are discussing virtue and romance. Lord Darlington states, "We are all in the gutter, but some of us are looking up at the stars." Therein lies your challenge. You are in the gutter with the rest of us. Human life has us all wallowing around in the gutter, laboring to make a living, raising children, paying bills and mulling our way through the dozens of boring mundane tasks of everyday life. And yet when we take time to look up at the stars, we realize our dreams lie there. The life we're *supposed* to be living waits for us there.

There's something you came here to do on earth, something significant and powerful. You are alive at this time in history because the world has desperate need of your talent, gift or perspective. You have something to say that's never been said. You have something to do that's never been done, or something to write that's never been written. There's a power that resides within you awaiting your discovery. It is rising up and calling on you to pay attention. And it will not let you rest or be happy until you make use of it and realize your dreams.

According to the Gospel of Thomas, Jesus said, "If you bring forth what is within you, what you bring forth will save you. If you do not bring forth what is within you, what you do not bring forth will destroy you." He was talking about this intense and powerful presence that lies within you. It is the power of you! And if you bring it forth, if you allow it entrance into your life by following your dreams, it will save you. It will save you from poverty, addiction, misery and loneliness.

However, if you do *not* bring it forth, if you don't allow the talent or wisdom you possess within to come out, this power is so persistent that it will not let you rest. It will create barriers and obstacles in front of you to direct you away from ego pursuits. Nothing you accomplish on your own will bring satisfaction. Inevitably, if you continue to persist in ignoring the power within you, it will turn inward on itself and destroy the outlet it created for its own expression: your body. Power that is released and circulated flourishes and grows. Power confined stagnates and destroys.

It's time to awaken to your power and assume the position life has in store for you. You have been designed by nature as a conscious co-creator. You have been given a gift. You have been set free on a journey of self-discovery. It's time to take your first steps.

The first step on your journey is to find your place in the scheme of things. Where do you fit in? Why are you here? For what purpose were you created? Out of the billions of people in our world, what makes you unique? To answer these questions, you have to start with a greater understanding of life itself. If you're going to have a bigger life, you have to start with a greater God.

My attempt in writing this book is to radically change the way you view your life and your relationship with the Creator. It is to introduce you to a new concept of God, not as an external deity, but as an indwelling presence. It is to help you appreciate and understand those inner urges you have for self-expression.

For reasons of expanding your concept of the Creator, I use many different words to describe the nature of God.

Spirit, Power, Creator, the Infinite and others all refer to the sacred and holy Presence that dwells within. On occasion I will use the word *It*. This is meant as no disrespect, but because of the limitations of the English language. We have no word to describe a presence that is neither male nor female.

the

Power

of

You

one

A Bigger Universe— a Greater God

The universe is really big, and really old. How big and how old? Well, according to the prevailing model known as the Big Bang, the universe began in an extremely dense phase called the Planck epoch, a state in which all matter and energy was concentrated. Imagine everything in the universe, every planet, galaxy and star reduced to the size of a pinpoint.

From that point, believed to be about thirteen billion years ago, the universe started to expand. The explosion of space, time and matter was so powerful that the expansion of the universe still continues today, even though it began billions of years ago.

According to scientists, the observable universe has a di-

ameter of ninety-three billion light-years. To gain an understanding of how large that is, all you have to do is multiply
the speed that light travels in a second (186,000 miles) by the
number of seconds in ninety-three billion years. And if
you're a *Star Trek*–watching, left-brain geek like I am, you
might have even considered getting out your calculator just
to see how many zeros are at the end of that number. It's
mind-blowing!

And then the question remains: Is this the *first* universe
ever created?. Or is it the hundredth or millionth? When his
holiness the Dalai Lama was asked if he understood the Big
Bang theory he responded, "Oh yes, I understand. But it's
not just one bang. It's bang, bang, bang."

Perhaps multiple universes exist simultaneously, all lay-
ered on top of each other like the skin of an onion. Or perhaps there are parallel universes, each one having its own
reality. Or maybe only one universe is created at a time, expanding for a few billion years and then contracting. Whatever the case, we now know that the universe is much larger
than we ever imagined. And it seems that whatever or whoever created it is intent on its continued existence.

Try to imagine the power that created and sustains the
universe. Is it completely impersonal, mathematically and
mechanically creating, or does it have some personal motivation? Is that power conscious of itself, specifically choos-

ing the design of every planet and species? Or is creation just a random act, unconsciously unfolding without a motivation or destiny?

To understand the power of you, you have to start by considering the power of the universe. Einstein said the most important question a person can ask is: "Is the universe a friendly place?" What intelligence is at the helm of the universe directing its activity? Is that intelligence friendly? In other words, does it like you?

Science can't answer these questions for us. It can only calculate, postulate and theorize. To dig deeper into the meaning of life and the power that sustains it, we have to turn to religion. The problem is, we have never really updated or modernized our religious beliefs, so our concept of God is still very primitive. Even though we have advanced in literally every other area of human study, religion has us stuck in the Dark Ages.

The Old Man in the Sky

Beware of the tiny gods frightened men create.

—HAFIZ,
fourteenth-century Sufi poet

I have a deeply religious friend who attended an orthodox church for more than twenty years. One week, after hearing the preacher give a sermon on Sunday morning about the evils of homosexuality, she made an appointment with him. My friend's son is gay and she wanted to ask her pastor: What kind of God loves some people and not others? Why would God go to all of the trouble to create someone that he found offensive? What purpose would it serve?

She did not get answers that satisfied her heart. She told me, "I had to leave that church because my God was too big for them." She could no longer worship a God whose love was so conditional. She couldn't believe in a God that would reward some with love and acceptance, and yet condemn others to eternal suffering and pain. "How could God be so judgmental and cruel?" she asked.

Many people have asked similar questions: If only Christians go to heaven, as some churches teach, what happens to the nearly one billion Hindus or the one and a half billion Muslims? Are they all misguided fools destined for hell? And since the universe is such a vast place, is it even reasonable to think we are the *only* intelligent life-forms that exist? And if not, what happens to the ETs? Are they doomed as well?

Because most societies on earth have been dominated by men for at least the last two thousand years, our image of God has always been male. He was created in the image and likeness of mortal man, equipped with all the trappings of the male ego.

Like most guys I know, it seems the old man in the sky likes to blow stuff up. But instead of those little green plastic army men that I used to blow up with firecrackers when I was a boy, God uses *real* men and *real* ammunition. So he's always up for a holy war, watching from on high, rooting for one side to win over another. Songs were written for him: *Onward, Christian soldiers, marching as to war.*

And what does the male ego need more than anything? Strokes! So the male God, up there in the sky, demanded to be worshiped and served. Of his own admission, he is a *jealous* god.

Instead of being created in the image and likeness of God, it seems as though we have created a God in *human* likeness, prone to emotional outbursts and character flaws. He is judgmental and inconsistent. And although he is known for acts of great love and forgiveness, so is he known for acts of incredible cruelty and violence. His personal tastes are unpredictable and confusing. While he appears to listen to and honor some prayers, he also ignores others.

I believe it's time to rid ourselves of the Old Testament, Zeus-like deity. The old-man-in-the-sky must die. In order for us to progress as a people and create a more peaceful world, we have to give up the idea of a regional god with personal preferences. He is primitive and outdated. Just as we once believed the earth was flat, later to discover we were quite wrong, it's time to let go of the belief in an external deity who lives on high waiting to judge and condemn.

I remember the disappointment I felt as a child when I learned there is no Tooth Fairy. My worldview was suddenly shattered, not to mention losing the only source I had for income. A few years later, all of my fantasies were further crushed when I was told there is no Santa Claus either. As children we cling to the idea of fantasy and magic. But as we grow and mature, we learn to accept the harsh reality that if there's going to be magic, we're going to have to make it ourselves.

If you decide, like my friend, to get a "bigger" God, some of the people around you will be upset. Your spiritual growth will appear blasphemous to them. They will recite their Bibles and promise his wrath. They will threaten you with damnation. They will use the most practiced and useful tools religion has had for centuries to manipulate and modify human behavior: fear and guilt. When it was believed the earth was flat and a few brave men courageously set sail to discover the new world, you can be certain there were those at the dock saying, "You're all going to die! You're going to fall off the ends of the earth."

Resistance is commonplace when progress is made and a new idea is introduced. There were those who said, "If man were meant to fly, he'd have wings." It sounds silly today, but it was once believed that the invention of the automobile would cause us all to go insane. Some said that the human body was not designed to move that quickly and that our minds weren't equipped to handle the intensity of movement. So, certainly when it comes to a concept as deeply ingrained in our culture as the Creator of the universe, resistance to change is to be expected.

Those who resist change will cling to the Bible as their backup authority. They will tell you it is a holy book. However, the Bible is not just a book. It's actually a library of ancient books. It was never meant to be the *final* word on God or religion. It was the *beginning* word, written thousands of years ago by primitive, tribal people. And though it is filled with great wisdom, it shouldn't be taken literally, nor should it be deified as the *only* source for spiritual knowledge. To do so stunts our growth spiritually and prevents us from maturing.

There are many sacred texts from other religions that hold great wisdom as well, such as the Bhagavad Gita from the Hindus, the Koran from the Islamic religion and the Sutras of Buddhism. Gather spiritual wisdom wherever you find it, but don't be trapped into thinking the one you may have grown up with is the *only* source. And always keep in mind that what you are reading was not written for our time.

Like many others, perhaps you're outgrowing your concept of God. Maybe it's time to expand your awareness of the power that created the universe. Maybe, like my friend, you need a bigger God, one big enough to love everyone, one compassionate enough to forgive everything and one powerful enough to create the cosmos.

In Him, We Live

> *It is your destiny to see as God sees, to know as God knows and to feel as God feels.*
>
> —MEISTER ECKHART,
> *thirteenth-century theologian*

I grew up in a small town in Kansas. Like morally centered, good Midwestern people, my parents and all three of their children attended the local Methodist church. I still remember some of those early Sunday school lessons, particularly the ones that baffled me. One of them came from the Book of Acts. The teacher tried to explain the quote "In him, we live and move and have our being" to a room full of seven-year-olds.

My concept of God at the time was an anthropomorphic

male deity who blessed some and cursed others based on their behavior, much like Santa Claus. On good days when everything was going well for me, I would think, "Well, I must be in the *heart* of God." But on bad days, when everything really stunk, I'd think, "Well, today I must be in God's butt." Kids take things *literally*, so be careful what you say.

My immature mind couldn't comprehend God as a Spirit or Intelligence. I just thought we were all floating around somewhere inside God's physical body. And some of us were in the good parts and some of us were in the really smelly parts, depending on whether he liked you or not.

As funny as it may seem, I can actually pinpoint the day in my life when my ideas about God and the universe started to change. It was September 8, 1966. That's when the first episode of *Star Trek* went on the air. And even though I was fascinated with Lieutenant Uhura, the character I most related to was Commander Spock. I loved his logic and sense of detachment from all of those messy feelings that ordinary humans get trapped in. I guess that was a sign I was going to be more left-brain than right.

Two years before *Star Trek* aired its first episode, in 1964, an Irish physicist named John Stewart Bell created what's known today as Bell's theorem. Through his experiments and the thousands that have been done since then, Bell determined something that Mr. Spock would have only one word for: fascinating!

Bell's theorem says that if distant objects have once been in contact with each other, a change in one causes an immediate change in the other. And here's the fascinating part: This change automatically occurs in the other object no matter how far apart they are, even if they're on complete opposite ends of the universe.

So what does this prove? Well, basically it means that the Intelligence in the universe must be one nonlocal being, meaning that what's known in one location is also known in every location simultaneously. And not only is this Intelligence nonlocal in distance, it's also nonlocal in time.

Get this: Scientific studies at Princeton University have shown that one person can influence the outcome of random physical events and can mentally convey complex information to another person even if they're on opposite ends of the planet.

And here's the freaky part: Studies show that not only can the sender mentally transmit detailed information to the receiver on the other side of the planet, the receiver can get the information up to three days *before* it was sent! So, not only is this universal Intelligence nonlocal in space. It's also nonlocal in time. Maybe that's the meaning of that other Bible quote from Isaiah that used to confuse me: "*Before* they call, I will answer."

The eighteenth-century French author Voltaire is quoted as saying, "God is a circle whose center is everywhere and circumference nowhere." Bell's theorem proved that. The universe is filled with a single Intelligence that is conscious in every location simultaneously. We are surrounded and immersed, like a fish in water, by the conscious intelligence of God.

You might say: In him, we live and move and have our being, except God is not a *him*. It's a Presence, not a person. It's a Spirit, not a man. It's an indwelling Presence, not an external deity.

An American Way of Thinking

> *I think that this—the United States of America—is still the most powerful economy in the world. It is an incredible engine for creativity and innovation. And it has the smartest, most effective workforce in the world.*
>
> —JAY CARNEY,
> *Obama administration press secretary*

I might be displaying a bit of national pride, but I happen to agree with what the White House press secretary said about our country. America has always been known for innovation. The very notion of a country established *for* the people and *by* the people was iconoclastic for its time. We have a unique culture of creativity in America that produces innovators and supplies the world with cutting-edge products. And even though China's economic growth intimidates the global economy and threatens to change the manufacturing industry in America, they have yet to produce a Steve Jobs or Mark Zuckerberg.

Without the weight of centuries of war and religious dispute, America has been perfectly poised to incorporate new ideas and bring them from conception to manifestation in record time. And this isn't just true of consumer goods and products. It is also true in matters of social change and spiritual philosophy.

One of the most famous American philosophers, Ralph Waldo Emerson, wrote an essay in the mid-nineteenth century entitled "Self-Reliance," in which he said, "We lie in the lap of immense intelligence, which makes us organs of its activity and receivers of its truth." This new and innovative approach to our relationship with the Creator spawned the Transcendentalist movement in America and caused a revolution in human consciousness.

Other spiritual philosophers would follow in the next century to build on Mr. Emerson's foundation. One of them, named Dr. Ernest Holmes, wrote, "Your soul belongs to the universe. Your mind is an outlet through which the Creative Intelligence of the universe seeks fulfillment." Thousands of people flocked to hear Dr. Holmes's lectures, which he began by announcing, "There is a Power for good in the universe that is greater than you are, and you can use it."

I believe the time has come for a new concept of spirituality to emerge, one that will eclipse old-world religions. And I believe it has already been born in America.

It's easy to imagine primitive man, thousands of years ago looking up to the stars from a dark and mysterious world wondering about the nature of life. They had unanswered questions such as: Why does lightning strike the earth and the sky grow so dark at night? Why do the winds blow strongly and destroy our homes? What makes the earth cold in one season and warm in another? What force controls these events?

Without an understanding of natural recurring weather patterns, primitive man looked up from the earth into the sky and assumed there must be somebody in charge. With so many things to control, it seemed unreasonable that only one god could be capable of handling them all. So numerous gods were born.

In Greek mythology, the gods of the sky and weather were named "Theoi Meteoroi." They were under the command of Zeus, the king of all gods. Aeolus was the god of the winds, appointed to guard violent storms which he kept locked away, releasing them to wreak havoc at the request of Zeus. He was just one of at least a dozen other gods responsible for everything from placing the morning dew to hanging a rainbow after a storm.

The human mind is very creative and will always seek to explain what is happening in the world. So primitive men created the gods in their image. They imagined deities that lived just beyond the clouds who were personally invested in human affairs. Each god was subject to human emotions and unpredictable behavior. Like us, the gods had the capacity for kindness and compassion and yet could also be quite cruel. To gain favor and appease the gods, temples were erected, rituals were performed and religion was born.

In time our paradigm of the universe and what forces were in control of our fate were radically altered. A new idea was born, erasing the concept of multiple gods and replacing it with just one. Yet even then, this new single god remained subject to human frailties of character and emotion. One day, he got so angry that he flooded the entire planet, nearly destroying everything on the earth. The next, he showed regret and promised to never repeat such a cruel act.

Billions of people in our world today still worship this god. They think of God as a male deity who decides each person's fate based on behavior. They pray to him, seeking personal gain and favor. They believe he has preferences, liking some people more than others or one sports team better than another. Though we have seen major advances in every other area of twenty-first-century life, we are still dragging around an outdated and archaic concept of God.

Our past religions have served us well. They have developed our moral character. They have parented our core values. They have inspired us to love one another and helped us become more civilized. But they have also deeply divided our society through rigid doctrines, pitting one group against another. And this divisive approach to religion continues to spawn the world's violence and terrorism.

We have come to the breaking point, the end of what once worked. We can no longer argue that one religion is right and the others are wrong. We desperately need a new idea, a new understanding of our placement in life and how to relate to our Creator, one that's inclusive of all people and respecting of every culture. The time has come for us to update our thinking about God and expand our awareness of the power that creates and sustains life.

This new inclusive spirituality and expanded awareness of what God is has to emerge from American soil. We are a land of free thinkers. We are pioneers intent on self-reliance. We're not bound by the weight of millennia of doctrine, religious dogma and ritual, so we're freer than anyone to embrace a new idea. America will have to lead the way, as it has done in the past, to change and transform the old world into the new.

THE SEVEN WHAT IFS

1. What if God isn't mad at you?
2. What if God isn't a judgmental old man recording everything you do wrong?
3. What if the Creator's only desire is for you to be fully expressed in love and joy?
4. What if your life has a purpose and a reason?
5. What if you have a talent that no one else can possess?
6. What if the universe is friendly and there's nothing operating against you?
7. What if your happiness and fulfillment in life is dependent upon nothing outside you?

A Conscious Connection to the Divine

Ah, but a man's reach should exceed his grasp, or what's a heaven for?

—ROBERT BROWNING,
"Andrea Del Sarto"

When Michelangelo painted Adam's outstretched hand reaching upward toward heaven to touch God, he mimicked a deep desire within the human spirit to connect with the Divine. There is some kind of homing device within our spirit that compels us to find our way back to the Source of life. Our shared, human dream is that one day we will have all that we want. One day, we will feel what it's like to be loved unconditionally and understood completely. One day, we will never have to worry whether there will be enough resources to sustain us. This deep desire within us will not let us fully rest until we find our happiness and enjoy the life of our dreams.

Because we think of ourselves primarily as *physical* beings with limited resources, we try to fulfill this deep longing within our soul externally in the world. Too many of us have sought self-fulfillment through material success, only to find the pleasure we experience fleeting and temporary. People come and go in our lives, careers end, and assets lose their value. In time, and sometimes through experiencing a great deal of personal loss, we finally turn to matters of spirit for fulfillment. And like Michelangelo's painting of Adam, we reach upward to find our God.

In ancient days, this desire to connect with God was ritualized. Animal sacrifices were burned at the altar, thinking God would be pleased by the scent. What man doesn't like a good barbecue, right? The intention was to gain God's favor so that good would flow more freely, the harvest would be more abundant and the weather less harsh. In more barbaric cultures, human sacrifices were made with the assumption that the greatest sacrifice would warrant the greatest reward. These early attempts were primitive at best and manipulative at worst.

In time, the two most popular ways to bridge the gap between humanity and Divinity emerged. Prayer was our first attempt to open a dialogue with God to plead our case and ask for favor. The spiritually immature prayed for personal gain. The spiritually mature prayed to align their will with God's will, understanding the natural order of life is to unfold the highest good for all. Meditation became the second resource for connection. Through quieting the monkey chatter of the human mind, it is thought that one can more clearly hear the call of the Divine and feel the oneness of life. Prayer and meditation became the two most common spiritual practices, and still are today.

However, as long as we think of God as an external deity instead of an internal presence, there will always be a great distance between us. Perhaps that is why Jesus and many other spiritual masters in their own language and culture said, "The kingdom of heaven is within." They advised us to look *inward* for our connection to a greater life, not out into the world, or up into the sky.

Inscribed in the forecourt of the Temple of Apollo in ancient Greece were the words, "Know Thyself." In Greek culture, it was believed that self-awareness would lead to peace and fulfillment and even perhaps to a discovery of our own Divine nature. This new approach proposed that we have looked too far away for God. Perhaps the God we go in search of up there in the heavens has never been farther from us than our breath. Perhaps Divinity is a seed planted in every human soul.

American philosopher Dr. Ernest Holmes wrote, "The thing you're looking for is the thing you're looking with," meaning the God we go in search of beyond the cosmos is the same God that lives as and through us. Dr. Holmes proposed that although each person is unique in personality and physical appearance, the same Spirit lives inside of us. This Spirit is the cause and Creator of life, and that which sustains it in all of its individual forms.

This new approach to spirituality changes how we connect to God. Instead of prayers of beseeching and pleading for our cause, it invites a more mindful approach to living and a conscious awareness of the Divine nature in everything that surrounds us. Instead of posing and performing for a God who watches from a distance, waiting to judge us, spiritual practice becomes a sincere attempt to recognize the Divine nature in all things. The Sanskrit word *Namaste* is used in modern times as a greeting that mirrors this idea: "I honor the Spirit in you, which is also in me."

With a less distant God, spiritual practice begins to take on a new tone, one that is less prescribed by religious doctrine or ancient ritual. For some it is practicing the art of mindfulness, keeping conscious of the simple things each day. The touch of a loved one's hand becomes a direct connection to Spirit. The beauty in a spring flower is seen as the presence of God. All of Nature is alive and contains a spiritual force.

Some Native American tribes believed the land in which they lived was holy and filled with the Great Spirit. Every day was spent in God's presence. Every mountain range and desert was hallowed. Every animal was sacred. Everything, they felt, was connected in one colossal web of life sustained by the Creator.

Some people mimic God's *creative* nature. To them, making art, singing or dancing is a spiritual practice. It invites God's creativity to be expressed through the individual. They see it as the ultimate act of surrendering ego to a Divine agenda. Through self-expression they touch the higher self within.

For people of a different nature, just listening to music or practicing yoga can be a spiritual practice. Fishing or camping under the stars can be a way to connect to God for some. Community and social activity is also a valid spiritual practice. There are as many inroads to Spirit as there are people on the planet. None are superior to others.

Resist the pressure of the crowd to prescribe how you choose to connect with Spirit. Follow your own instinctive nature. Authenticity should be your only compass. If something feels contrived and unnatural, it's probably not the best way. Find a spiritual practice that *feels* right and commit to it regularly.

Jumping Through Hoops for Jesus

I confess. I have a guilty summer pleasure. It's watching *America's Got Talent* on television. I love to see all of the unusual acts. The judges on the show are assigned the grueling task of having to filter through the people with no talent except to embarrass themselves, to find the needle in the haystack, the ones who have *real* talent. It amazes me what some are willing to do publicly, in front of millions of people. I prefer to keep my imagined talents private so there can be no permanent record of me singing in the shower or dancing in the kitchen on YouTube. But clearly others don't think as I do. Maybe that's what makes the show so entertaining.

On one show, a woman had trained her dog to jump through hoops surrounded by fire. Unfortunately, when the dog was in front of the large audience, not even a marinated beef snack could entice him to perform. He just looked up at her with one of those looks that seems to say, "Are you crazy, lady? I'm not jumping through those hoops."

I feel the same way as that lady's dog. I can't believe in a God that would have me jumping through hoops just to gain favor. What kind of cruel deity would sit on high being entertained by humanity's folly? Certainly not an Intelligence that creates a universe.

Nor can I believe in a God who would use disease or suffering as a tool to teach lessons or modify behavior. That's not how we teach our own children. We don't expose them to some harmful pathogen to make them sick so they will learn their lessons in school. Nor do we put up obstacles for them to overcome so they can gain our love and acceptance. What kind of diabolical plan would that be?

I got clear a long time ago that I am not here to suffer. I will not jump through hoops to prove my worth. I will not go through hell to get to heaven. I will not suffer through pain or misery to be purified. There can be no intelligent or loving God who would require such a thing.

Many religions are fond of saying that God is love. And yet their God doesn't act in a very loving manner. I believe that God is *perfect* love, and that means it gives itself without expectation or requirement. God's love is unconditional, undeniable and readily available to all, regardless of their past experience or current condition.

God isn't a loving deity who sends love down to earth from his storehouse up in heaven. God is love itself. It lives in us as our own capacity for love, compassion and forgiveness. And that means love doesn't come *from* other people. It comes *through* them. There is only one Source for love, and that is love itself.

Get it out of your head right now that you are here to jump through hoops to prove you are worthy of receiving your good. There is no God in the universe that requires it. Nor are you required to pay your dues by going through hell to get to heaven. There is no virtue in suffering. No one has ever been made better by it. No one's life has ever been improved by it. Anything you learned from suffering, you could have just as easily learned from being happy.

The universe and the Power that sustains it is on your side. It always has been. The only thing God wants for your life is the same thing all parents want for their children: They want them to be happy. They want them to be loved. They want them to find peace and fulfillment.

You are not here to prove yourself to anyone, especially the Creator. Stop jumping through hoops. Stop posing for Jesus. The universe is not impressed with pretense. It is indifferent to your impersonations.

Relocating God

I had a guest on my radio show a few years ago who shared the story of his spiritual transformation. He had left his childhood religion behind in favor of a more inclusive spirituality. And because of that, he found himself caught between two religious paradigms, one that worshiped a distant deity and another that practiced the presence of Spirit within.

That's the challenge for everyone who grows spiritually beyond the concept of God as an old-man-in-the-sky. If there's no God "up there" to worship, if God isn't a deity who lives somewhere just beyond earth's atmosphere, then what is it and *where* is it?

Poet and American philosopher Henry David Thoreau wrote: "Nature is full of genius, full of the divinity; so that not a snowflake escapes its fashioning hand." We look too far away for miracles. We seek power from external sources when the power to choose our destiny is within our own reach. We seek to gain fortune from others by exchanging our time and effort for their resources. And yet our greatest riches can come only from following the talent that's been placed within us by our Creator. When we're confused, we run around asking other people what to do instead of con necting to the Source of all wisdom within our own mind.

The good you seek from others has been left inside you to discover. The God you go in search of up there in the sky is present here on earth. It has not abandoned its creation. It lives inside of you. It is guiding you toward life-fulfillment through your dreams. It is pointing you toward your destiny by providing your mind with new ideas. It will lead you to love if you'll just follow your heart.

We approach life as though we are powerless victims, when the truth is, we are powerful co-creators. We are already in partnership with the Divine. It is the Intelligence within our bodies causing them to breathe and circulate our blood. It is the Life within our cells regenerating and creating billions of new ones every day just so we can stay alive. It is the Wisdom in our minds that we access through our thoughts. It is the Love in our hearts that allows us to feel. God is not an external deity, it's an internal Presence. It is an indwelling Spirit that occupies every living thing.

This new paradigm will challenge your relationship with God and change how you approach life. At first it will feel awkward to pray. It will seem silly to pose. If no one up there is listening or watching, what's the use? When you take God out of the sky and place it down here in your life, everything changes. Going to church and reciting old scriptures may lose its meaning for you. You will have to find a new way to sense the Presence and connect to the Power that can create an entire universe out of thin air.

Two Paths to God

Contrary to what most religions promote, there are as many paths to God as there are people on the planet. No religion has the exclusive on an Infinite Presence. Like spokes on a wheel that all converge at the center, we are on our own individual path to enlightenment. And the good news is: We will find what we're looking for on the path we're on. There is no *wrong* path or *futile* effort when it comes to your spiritual journey. Every man who seeks will find. Every woman who knocks will have the door opened to her. The Spirit we go in search of *wants* to be found. And It's not far away.

Several of the world's mystics have pointed to the two most common paths to God: The path of wisdom and the path of love. It's easy to tell which path you are on. Use the guide on the following pages to determine for yourself.

IF YOU ARE ON THE PATH OF WISDOM, YOU:

- Have read just about every self-help book there is
- Have a large library of books on various topics from spirituality to science
- Are fascinated by new technologies and scientific discoveries
- Value and respect wisdom in others
- Tend to be more aware of your thoughts than your feelings
- Enjoy mind games and puzzles
- Keep yourself mentally alert and stimulated
- Are methodical
- Tend to be organized and sometimes fastidious

IF YOU ARE ON THE PATH OF LOVE, YOU:

- Value relationships with family and/or friends more than anything else
- Have empathy toward others in hardship or pain
- Practice compassion
- Get your heart broken easily

- Have difficulty passing homeless people on the street without giving
- Are easily moved by heartfelt stories or shows on television
- Might be an artist or performer
- Don't like competition
- Respect and value others who feel as deeply as you do

Regardless of which path you are on, it is the right one for you. Follow it faithfully and it will lead to your answers. You are not alone on your path. Others are like you. Seek them out. Together you will grow more quickly.

It is also common to start your spiritual journey on one path and then switch to another, or go back and forth. Every road leads to self-awareness. Every step on the path has value. There are no straight lines to God, only a zigzag journey. Life is more adventurous that way.

A New Way to Pray—
A Better Way to Live

Without a God up there in the sky to beseech, prayer becomes less of an *ask* and more of an acceptance. Instead of a passive appeal, it is more of an active experience. Nearly two thousand years ago, the Roman emperor Marcus Aurelius wrote a prayer that still serves as a great example today.

THE PRAYER OF MARCUS AURELIUS

Everything harmonizes with me
which is harmonious to thee, O Universe.

Nothing for me is too early or too late
which is in due time for thee.

Everything is fruit to me
which thy seasons bring, O Nature.

From thee are all things,
in thee are all things,
to thee are all things.

In his prayer, he refers to the Creator using the words *Universe* and *Nature*, both of which imply a Presence, not a person. His prayer is not an ask for something, but an affirmation and acceptance of the natural order. His prayer begins with a recognition of a Power greater than himself, but yet of the same nature. He writes, "Everything harmonizes with me which is harmonious to thee, O Universe." It is a statement that he and God (Universe) are in peaceful alignment with each other.

Next he writes, "Nothing for me is too early or too late which is in due time for thee." How many times have you prayed with an urgent need? For some people, the only time they actually do pray is when their need is so desperate that they can't think of anything else to do. I can't tell you how many times I lay in bed at night when I was a kid in trouble begging, "Help me, Jesus!" However, in this prayer Marcus Aurelius recognizes that everything in the universe has a sequence. Everything unfolds according to spiritual law and Divine order.

"Everything is fruit to me which thy seasons bring, O Nature." This is also an acceptance that everything in life happens for a reason and that the purpose of Nature is to always unfold the highest good, regardless of appearances. The winters look dark and dreary. Nothing seems to be growing. The trees lose their leaves, the grass is brown and the sky is gray. And yet Nature springs to life again. This part of the prayer reminds us to not judge by the way things appear. Nature has a plan. Trust that a higher good is unfolding regardless of what appears in your life today.

In the final part of his prayer, Marcus Aurelius recognizes the unity of life and the oneness of our being. He states, "From thee are all things, in thee are all things, to thee are all things." This is another way of saying, "In him, we live and move and have our being." It is a recognition that there's only one Power in the universe and it is the Source of all good.

EXERCISE:
A GREATER GOD

Practice writing your own prayers without asking for anything or trying to negotiate a deal with God. Use common language. Don't try to be religious. Start, as Marcus Aurelius did, with a recognition that everything in life is in harmony and unfolding toward the greatest good. The purpose of your prayer is not to get God to *do* something. It is to make you more aware of what God is *already* doing.

All of this may seem new to you at first. Be patient with yourself as you transition from worshiping a distant deity to embracing a spiritual Presence within. In the beginning, your prayers might be half beseeching and half affirming. That's okay. Just keep praying and you will discover there's power within you that has been waiting for your recognition. That power is unlimited in its scale and personally invested in your life. You can partner with it to make your dreams come true.

two

Self-Discovery

I want to share my own story with you because I believe in some way everyone's story is part of the greater story of humanity, each of us in our own individual way, just trying to discover our true self.

Somehow by a very young age, I learned that I'm not going to be good enough. Maybe the message came from a family member, or a kid at school, or maybe I just absorbed it from the negative culture we live in. Whatever the case, the message was received loud and clear: You are not good enough!

By second grade, I learned that I couldn't make it as an artist, because I had no skills at drawing or painting. By fifth grade, all it took was one PE class to learn that Nature had not designed my body for athletic endeavors. By sixth grade, I was being bullied by the other boys in school. Maybe that's why in seventh grade I started using drugs.

I used to smoke pot every day in an alleyway across the street from school. When that didn't satisfy me, I started taking these tiny little pills called "white cross" before typing class. It was amazing how much faster I could type on amphetamines.

At thirteen, I got high on purple microdot acid at a Led Zeppelin concert. The year was 1970 and the drug culture was in full force. At fourteen, in eighth grade, I got kicked out of school. The principal caught me smoking Marlboros on campus.

Finally by twelfth grade, my self-destructive behavior was more than just a part-time endeavor. It was a well-established full-time habit. By then the message was so deeply engrained in my psyche that I repeated it over and over again in my own head even when others had stopped saying: You are not good enough!

By the time I turned twenty years old, my self-destruct button had been pushed so many times the lettering on it wore off. I was drinking heavily, doing drugs and waking up with strangers in my bed, not remembering who was lying next to me, or how we both got there. That was the unfortunate side effect of taking quaaludes: short-term memory loss, which was great if you didn't want to remember what you did the night before because you were too ashamed.

The truth be told: I was miserable. I was unhappy, dissatisfied with everything in life and searching; constantly searching for something or someone to make me feel good about myself. There was a desperate longing in my soul that I kept trying to satisfy with anything that would make me happy, even if that happiness was short-lived.

And then by accident, coincidence or Divine appointment, whichever you prefer, I walked into a spiritual center one Sunday morning and heard a message I'd never heard before. It went something like this: *You are perfect just as you are right now. God loves you completely without judgment or condition.*

I didn't believe it. I *wanted* to believe it, but I didn't. In fact, I was pretty sure God *didn't* love me as I was and I was damn sure no one else would. So I decided to put myself on a course of self-improvement. I found the perfect teacher for me, a spiritual leader named Dr. Kennedy Shultz, and I enrolled in every class he offered.

I learned about Emerson and Thoreau and the rest of the American Transcendentalists. I read just about every book in the self-improvement section of the bookstore. And in time, my self-image started to change. I was feeling better about myself. Some of the self-destructive behavior stopped, not all of it, but *some* of it. I wasn't doing drugs anymore but I was still having sex with too many anonymous partners.

My self-improvement strategy was in full force. I took every self-help class or workshop offered. I studied world religions and philosophy. I became a licensed prayer practitioner so I could help others get what they wanted out of life. I got a better job, drove a better car and lived in a better house. Everything was getting better. Everything that needed to be fixed in my life was getting fixed.

And my strategy paid off. The new and *improved* version of me was healthier, much happier and a lot nicer. And when I went to the spiritual center and heard the message that God loves me just as I am, this time I *believed* it. In fact, I started to brag about it to others. I mean why *wouldn't* God love me? I got it going on, baby!

But oddly enough, even after years of self-improvement, it was still there: this deep longing in my soul. In the quiet hours of the day, when all of the distractions were taken away and I was left alone with my thoughts, I still craved something and I couldn't figure out what it was.

"What more do you want?" I asked myself. "You have a better life, more friends and more money. What else could you possibly want?" No answer came. Nothing—just this deep sense that something else was missing. And then the thoughts returned, old ones I hadn't entertained in a long time. And the message was still loud and clear: You are not good enough!

In Greek mythology, the story is told of a Minotaur, a bull-headed, flesh-eating creature who lives at the center of a labyrinth. He's a huge, threatening beast. And yet, oddly enough, his name is Asterion, which means "star." It's a paradox. All great truths are wrapped in paradox.

Like the Minotaur, the thing that resides at the center of your being, at the very core of who you are, is a beast. It can destroy you. Or it can be what makes you a star and reveals your *true* self. And you won't know which one it is until you go there, to the center of your being inside the labyrinth to face the beast.

That's what this nagging sense of not being good enough was to me. It was the beast at the center of my being. And no matter how many trips I made around the *outside* of the labyrinth trying to avoid him, he would not stop rearing his ugly face. No matter how glossy the outside of my life was, on the *inside*, the beast was still there.

So instead of trying to avoid him, instead of trying to get him to shut up, this time, I *leaned* into my longing. I felt the sadness and emptiness in my soul that came from years of buying into the story that I'm not good enough, something I'd been trying to avoid doing for a long time.

And then I saw the beast. We came face-to-face with each

other. And that's when the epiphany came. I realized everything I'd been doing to improve myself, all of the classes I
took and the books I read on self-improvement, all of it was
just another strategy to fix what I believed was broken.

My motivation had never changed. The core belief was still
lodged inside: You are not good enough! I was just reacting to
it in a different way. Instead of anesthetizing it with drugs and
alcohol, I was *schooling* it, trying to *improve* it or *amend* it.
And all that did is put a shiny but thin veneer on top of it.

On the outside of my life, everything looked great. But
since the core belief had never changed, on the inside I still
longed for something that I could never put my finger on.
Later I discovered that what I was longing for is what every
soul longs for, a connection to Spirit, that Higher Self that
resides within, the God-self.

Most people aren't aware of this, but we each have a homing device implanted by our Creator. It was placed there so
we would always be able to find our way home. The homing
device is our own soul's longing for God, a deep and powerful need to connect to love, peace and joy.

No matter how you try to satisfy this longing by arrang-
ing things on the *outside* of your life, it will not let you rest
until you come to the *center*, the core of your being, to find
out who you really are. And it's there where you'll have to

face the Minotaur, the beast of lies you've been told and the anger and pain you feel for having believed them for so long.

As you face the beast and your fear that it will destroy you, you'll find that what doesn't destroy you somehow transforms you. And that's when the beast turns into a star and reveals your true self.

In nineteenth-century Victorian England, Oscar Wilde was sentenced to two years of hard labor in prison for being a homosexual. Left alone to rot and die in his cell, Mr. Wilde wrote "De Profundis," an extraordinary letter revealing the most profound truth that he'd come to know. Surely inside that cell he must have faced his own inner beast. This is what he wrote: "The final mystery is oneself. When one has weighed the sun in balance and measured the steps of the moon and mapped out the seven heavens, star by star, there still remains oneself."

Inevitably your spiritual journey will lead you back to yourself. You can look in a thousand other places for your good and spend a thousand years doing it, but eventually you'll have to go within and face who you are.

When you stop running from your own longing, you will discover that the longing itself will carry you to the core of your being, that place where you'll discover the truth of who you are. And from that moment on, you'll never again question your worth. Never again will you believe the lies you've been told.

We waste so much of our time here on earth searching "out there" for something to satisfy us. We spin our wheels trying to find happiness and satisfaction in life by manipulating outside events and worshiping external deities. And yet, ironically, in the last place on earth we ever think to look, the truth has been placed within us. The God we go in search of resides within.

Hitting the Wall

Sufi mystic and writer Llewellyn Vaughan-Lee wrote an essay titled "The Wall." To be published in his forthcoming book: *Darkening of the Light: Witnessing the End of an Era.* In it he wrote about the same experience I had, but in a little different way. He said:

> *In deep meditation I come to a wall. I know this wall. I have seen it many times before. . . . It is a high brick wall. I know what is on the other side of the wall: a world of light. But there is no way through; there is no doorway, no ladder, no break in the wall.*

Maybe you've reached your own impasse in your spiritual growth, as I did with recurring feelings of worthlessness. Maybe you've come to the wall and there doesn't appear to be any way around it. There's no open door and the wall is too high to scale. You can see the light on the other side of it and you know that's where you're *supposed* to be. But how do you get there? What do you do?

The secret is to stop clawing at the wall. Stop glossing it over and pretending it looks pretty. Go within and *lean* into your longing. Feel the loneliness in your heart for Spirit. It will lead you to the light. And if you do that, one day the wall will dissolve right before your eyes, revealing itself as just another false illusion.

There's something within you waiting to be born; a Power that screams at you every day, a voice inside your own heart that knows the truth. It's Spirit calling you to know yourself and to believe in yourself. And if you'll spend time listening to that voice, that high wall that's got you trapped behind it will start to crumble and you'll discover your *true* self; not the one that's been put down by society, but the one that's been set free by Spirit.

Just beyond the wall of low self-value, some people have to face the wall of fear. Conquering fear is the soul's greatest task and the next step on your journey to self-discovery.

What to Do with Fear

I must not fear. Fear is the mind-killer. Fear is the little-death that brings total obliteration. I will face my fear. I will permit it to pass over me and through me. And when it has gone past I will turn the inner eye to see its path. Where the fear has gone there will be nothing. Only I will remain.

—FRANK HERBERT,
Dune

As spiritual beings, temporarily housed in human bodies, we share a common bond and challenge. Each of us has to face our own fears. That is the big challenge set before us in human life. We have been left to discover the innate power and potential we hold inside as spiritual beings in a world rampant with fear. Resources appear to be scarce. Danger seems to lurk around every corner. Violence is embedded in our culture. Disease is an infectious and dramatic part of human life. Every day there seems to be something new to fear.

We're afraid we're not going to make it financially, or be able to support our families. We ask ourselves, "Where will the money come from? What happens if I get laid off from work?" We fear disease: "What if I get sick? Who will take care of me? Will there be enough money for health care?" We fear suffering. God forbid, something should happen and we fall victim to some horrible act of violence. We fear we're not good enough, that we just don't have it in us to succeed, or that we don't match up to other people. And then ultimately the biggest fear we have, the granddaddy of them all—fear of being alone. What if nobody loves me and I have to spend the rest of my life alone?

My grandmother was immobilized by fear. She was agoraphobic, which is a fear of being in public spaces. She exhibited classic symptoms. I remember visiting her house as a little boy, wondering why every door was locked, the shades pulled down and the curtains drawn. I didn't understand her self-imposed limitations. I couldn't figure out why she wouldn't go outside with me to play.

My grandmother never left the house. When she needed to see a dentist, she didn't go, so her teeth rotted and fell out. When my grandfather went into the hospital, she never visited. When he died, she didn't go to the funeral. She was scared to death of being in public, desperately afraid to step outside her door. For more than forty years, she remained locked up in that house, like a prisoner in a cell.

Fear is a gigantic monster that needs regular feedings to stay alive. The more you feed it, the bigger the monster grows. The more time and attention you give to fear, the more it takes from your life. The more you accommodate it by indulging in thinking about all of the things that scare the hell out of you, the smaller your life gets and the more trapped you are inside, just like my grandmother, imprisoned in her house for four decades.

Now, of course this doesn't happen all at once, or you would notice it. Fear is much more camouflaged, so it creeps into our lives a little bit at a time so it will go unnoticed. Like a thief in the night, it quietly enters.

Fear hates the daylight, so it usually comes by cloak of darkness to haunt. It arrives when you're not at the helm, when you're not really conscious of your own thinking. So one night, because you haven't stood watch at the doorway of your mind, before you know it, the thief has entered. And it has come to steal your faith and peace of mind.

It wakes you up in the middle of the night, usually around three or four in the morning, and, like a spoiled child, demands your attention. It wants to go over your finances. "Let's talk about your bank balance," it cries out. It wants to do a weigh-in to see how much you've gained. It wants to go over the list of things that *might* happen someday. Before you know it, an hour or two has passed and a lot of sleep has been lost.

Eventually the nightmare is over and you go back to sleep. You wake up the next day, thinking to yourself, "What a rough night. Thank God that's over." But the problem is, it's not. In fact, it's not over at all. The thief has just begun to steal from you.

Because you spent all of that time the night before feeding the monster, it has a hold over you now, and not in ways you'll easily recognize; more so in covert, hidden ways, just beneath the surface of your conscious awareness.

First it shows up in your decisions, in the choices you make about your life. Instead of living the extraordinary life of a Divine being, the bold and courageous life your Creator had in mind for you to live, you've become average. You go with the status quo. You make the safe choice, or at least the one that *appears* to be safe. Instead of pursuing your wildest dreams, the thing you really have passion for, you make the lesser choice, the one others are making, the safe one. And you tell yourself that's the smart choice: "After all, I have to be realistic. What kind of world would we be living in if everybody suddenly did what they wanted, if everyone just decided to pursue their dreams?"

But that's not *you* talking anymore; it's fear. It has stolen your faith in the night and taken away your passion. And now the thief is using your own tongue to wag up and down, spewing out rationalizations for accepting less.

That's how it starts, in the choices you make. Instead of choosing in faith, now you choose in fear. You make decisions about your career, health care, family, even about your church, all based in fear. Fear has taken hold of you and is working its way down in the decision-making process, from the most important choices you make about your life, down to the most trivial. Fear now decides where you're going to work, whom you're going to love and what part of town you will go into. It decides what you're going to say, when you're going to say it and how you will act. It even chooses what you're going to wear.

Before you know it, you've given your entire life over to fear and you're not even conscious you have done it. The thief has cleaned you out, gutted you from the inside out. It has taken your joy and passion for life. It has stolen your faith and left you with the one thing you will always have more of—fear!

Little by little, day by day, fear teaches you to lower your expectations. And then one day, all of those choices you've made in fear have solidified themselves into your belief system. Now you're not in control anymore. Fear is. And from then on, your life is just a repetitive cycle of believing something is so, and then creating evidence to support your belief.

You believe it's hard to find work after a certain age, and guess what? Now you have evidence to prove it. You believe no one is going to love you in the shape you're in, and guess what? You have evidence to prove it. You believe you're going to get sick again this year, about the same time you did last year, and guess what? Right on cue, you get sick.

Jesus said it simply: It is done unto you as you *believe*. So, your fear-based belief system creates the circumstances and conditions necessary to perfectly match your belief and draws them into your experience.

So now you've got evidence of your belief. Now you can say, "See, I told you!" And you can be self-righteous about it: "See, I told you I was too fat. Nobody's going to love me this way. See, I told you it was hard to get a job after fifty. See, I told you!" And that's how the very thing we fear the most comes upon us and how little by little, each day, we train ourselves to accept much less from life than we actually deserve.

But what if there was something that could help you with fear, something that could actually dissolve it and make it disappear? Well, there is. Like light does to darkness, there is one thing that completely obliterates all fear. It's the exact opposite of fear, its perfect nemesis. It's called love. And I'm not talking about romantic love, not the kind you feel for a mate or spouse. It's spiritual love or Divine Love that dissolves fear.

In the ancient text of Hinduism, the Bhagavad Gita, which literally translated means "the song of the beloved lord,"

Krishna is the supreme being, the one perfect life. He is described as the uncontainable, unchanging and all-pervading presence. Krishna is loved and worshiped by Hindus in a variety of forms, unlike the god Jehovah in the western Bible. Jehovah was the father figure, a male deity responsible for judgment, punishment and reward. Hindus see their God playing many different roles. Sometimes he is a mischievous child. At other times, he is a confidant or close friend. But his most common role is that of ultimate lover.

As the ultimate lover, Krishna is famous for his Divine Love call that he sends forth by a captivating and irresistible tone he plays on a flute. As this seductive and powerful melody is received, people everywhere drop what they're doing: leave their homes, abandon their work and follow the music. Eventually they break into a dance of Divine Love.

In the Bhagavad Gita, Krishna's call to love carries the most powerful message of this ancient text written hundreds of year before Christ. And that message is: The heart of God *passionately* desires to connect with the hearts of humans.

Now, perhaps the story of your life isn't as glamorous as the Bhagavad Gita. Maybe you're not going to hear God playing the flute and drop everything you're doing and break into dance. But nonetheless, you are still supposed to have an *intimate* and *personal* relationship with your Creator. And the benefits of that kind of relationship are amazing. By building a trust with God, you build your faith that whatever you desire will be provided. And by reinforcing that relationship each day with spiritual practice and prayer, you change your belief system. You realign it with the truth that then changes everything else in your life. So, instead of giving your attention to what you fear, as you did in the past, suddenly you find yourself more interested in what you have faith in, what brings you joy and ignites your passion.

You probably don't even know it, but you've already received the Divine Love call. It wasn't a flute playing. It was an urge within you to do something with your life, to make something of yourself, to use your talents and passion to create something of value to the world.

Spirit is calling. Can you hear it? Or has it been silenced by your fear? Something within you desires to be let out. Can you feel the urge? Or are you too busy entertaining your fears?

The Bible says: "Choose today whom you will serve." Every day you have to make a choice—will I follow the Divine Call to companionship? Will I pursue my best ideas, even when I can't see how they will manifest? Will I go forward in faith? Or will I cower in fear, huddle with the masses who keep pretending to be small and insignificant? Choose today.

Face Fear

I like to read about successful people. I'm fascinated by the stories of how they got where they are and what lessons they've learned along the way. You have to get interested in what you want in your own life. That's how you achieve it. So if you want to be a success, get interested in successful people. You can learn a lot from the people who've gone before you and maneuvered their way through life well.

One of my favorite stories is about the Academy Award–winning actress Helen Mirren. True to her English heritage, at a very young age, little Helen was sent away to boarding school. The British are known for liking their dogs more than their children, so they keep their dogs at home and send their children off to boarding school.

Well, young Helen was no exception, so at the tender age of ten years old, off she went to a school run by Bernardine nuns, who all wore these Darth Vader–like black robes and looked like the witches in the opening act of *Macbeth*.

On her very first day, she had to sit for an interview with the headmistress, who was a very old lady named Dame Mother Mary Mildred. And according to Helen's account of the story, Dame Mother Mary Mildred was not a very attractive woman. She had the misfortune of having one eye that drooped very badly. So it wasn't her looks that carried her through life. It was her wisdom. She was a very wise old woman.

So, this quivering, frightened little ten-year-old girl goes before the headmistress, who takes one look at Helen, peers her head over the desk, looking down through her drooped eye, and says one of those things you hear as a child and never forget. She said: "Beware of fear!"

Young Helen was so impressed by the theatrics of this event that it became her mantra for life. Those three words became the wisdom she used to build a successful career as an actress: *Beware of fear.* So when new creative opportunities would show up, Helen had the freedom to step out and take risks that others were too afraid to take. Unlike many others, she vowed to not let fear stand in her way.

Someone else said it a little differently but still used three words: "Be not afraid!" was the command Jesus gave to his disciples. Fear is the only enemy you will ever know. Fear is what stands between you and the life you really want to live. Fear is a poison that kills every good thing trying to make its way into your life.

The Thing You Fear the Most

A friend of mine is reaching the age where he's starting to plan for retirement, so he's doing everything he can to secure a comfortable future. He maximized his 401(k) contribu-tions. He purchased long-term-care insurance. He bought an annuity. He's doing all the things you're *supposed* to do to guarantee security. From a financial planner's perspective he's doing all the right things, and yet I'm not sure if he's do-ing them for the right reason.

The problem is, it's not just your actions that dictate your future. It's more the *motivation* behind them that is caus-ative. In other words, it's your consciousness, or belief sys-tem, that creates your experience. So, if you're planning a future based on what you *fear* might happen, guess what's going to happen—the very thing you feared the most. When this occurs people usually say: "See, it's a good thing I pre-pared for this, because look what happened." But what they don't know is that the thing they feared the most came to them *because* they prepared for it. They expected it. Their belief in the negative experience is actually what caused it to occur.

So I want to tell my friend, save your money, but don't save it for medical costs in case you get sick. Save it for a condo at the beach or to spend on a handsome lover in the Greek islands when you retire. Now, that's worth saving for, right? Can't you just see yourself at eighty years old, all wrinkled and rich, lying on a beach somewhere, being waited on hand and foot?

Be not afraid. Plan a future that excites you, one that invigorates you; one that's worthy of a spiritual being living in an unlimited universe. Set the vision for your future high, way up there, beyond where your fears can reach.

The Power of Vulnerability

The fearful are obsessed with trying to minimize risks and control events. It's security they're after. They don't like feeling vulnerable. This need for security is a national obsession that's taken over our lives since 9/11. For the first time in recent history, Americans realized we're actually quite vulnerable. We thought we were too powerful or too rich to be touched by the violence other nations deal with. We thought we were safely distanced from it. But on that September morning in 2001, we were rudely awakened by the reality of our own vulnerability. And I'm not sure our reaction to it has been all that healthy.

Are we safer as a nation? Are we more secure? I'll let you apply your own wisdom to answer those questions; that's not for me to say. But what I can say is, perhaps our actions should be driven less by fearful reaction and more by the wisdom of Dame Mother Mary Mildred who said: *Beware of fear!* As one bumper sticker I saw recently said: "We keep creating enemies faster than we can kill them."

Whether it's individually caused or collectively as a nation, the results are the same when our actions are motivated by fear. What they create is more of the very thing we fear the most. Perhaps what we really need to do to secure our nation is take the advice of a former president who said, "The only thing we have to fear is fear itself."

Like it or not, the universe has created us to be vulnerable. Our bodies can be pierced and bleed to death. Our hearts can be broken, our minds easily confused. We're *supposed* to be vulnerable. Nature has designed us this way because only when our hearts and minds are open are we truly worthwhile.

I remember my first crush in grade school. Her name was Jeanie. She was this cute little blond girl who sat across from me in class, flirting. She would toss her hair back and forth, bat her pretty blue eyes and just stare at me. I tried to ignore her for as long as I could. But then one day I started to talk with her and give her my attention. I was instantly enthralled. At twelve years old, I decided she was going to be my girlfriend and we were going to live happily ever after.

However, once she got to know me a little better, she decided she didn't like me very much and rejected me. In a matter of twenty-four hours, my entire life plan went kablooey. So, I decided, that's it! I'll never let myself be that vulnerable again. My heart was destroyed by puppy love.

I played Donny Osmond's record over and over, singing along: *And they called it puppy love*. I especially liked the part where he sang: *Someone help me, help me, help me, please*.

Looking back on it now, it does seem a bit melodramatic. But as juvenile as it was, my reaction was all too common. To some degree, that's what we all do when we get hurt: we back off, build up armor or insulate ourselves to console our pain. We eat comfort food and retreat into our emotional cave to avoid getting hurt again. We don't like feeling vulnerable.

I feel drawn to do that with global issues these days. I'm getting emotionally fatigued. There's just too much happening out there that breaks your heart, like the earthquake in Japan and the famine in Somalia. It's hard to see the devastation, to look into the numb faces on TV of those who've been affected by such tragedies. So my knee-jerk reaction is to turn it off and tune it out. I don't want to see it anymore.

I feel the same thing when I see homeless people on the street begging for money. I try not to make eye contact with them because I don't want to connect with their pain or loss. I don't want to feel what they feel. I don't want to see the hopelessness and despair in their eyes. So I look away or pretend I'm on my cell phone.

Gangaji, the author of *The Diamond in Your Pocket*, says we should do just the opposite. She wrote: "Whatever is here, despair, anger, or hopelessness, the opportunity is not to cover it up with denial, but to face it, to meet it, to directly experience it." She believes the only way we can be truly conscious in life is to be conscious of *everything*, not just the things that make us feel good, but also the pain and suffering in the world.

Only by facing our vulnerability and directly experiencing it are we able to get beyond it and see the truth underlying it; the truth that in the midst of all of this chaos, there is order. In the face of all of this violence, there is peace. When we open ourselves to both the joy and the sorrows of life, we realize that life is beautiful and ugly, tragic and inspiring.

By letting your heart break over and over again, you get to that part of yourself that's unbreakable. By connecting with the broken heart of humankind, you find the unbreakable heart of Spirit, which contains a deep love and compassion that erases all pain.

When I had my puppy love with Jeanie and got upset because she didn't like me back, I was afraid I'd get hurt again, so I insulated myself. I used anger as a strategy to not feel pain. Many people do that because it's a lot easier to stay mad than it is to feel the sadness of not getting your needs met.

It's a lot easier to insulate yourself, to comfort your loss with food or something else to avoid feeling. But in the end, it's a strategy that fails us all because we get trapped inside. And even though we have lots of insulation around us, we're still hurting inside, still just trying to avoid feeling the pain.

But what would happen if we just felt it? What if we just let our hearts break? What if we just accepted the fact that we can't control everything that happens, that sometimes life is uncertain and unpredictable? What would happen if we fully embraced our vulnerability? Maybe we would heal and be made whole again. Maybe we'd get to the other side of it.

Haven't you ever wondered how people like Mother Teresa can do what they do? What about those who work in the trenches of poverty and despair in Third World countries? How do they spend every day witnessing so much suffering and misery? How could you not be emotionally slayed by that? I think the secret is, instead of trying to avoid it or insulate themselves from the vulnerability of the situation, they just lean into it and let their hearts break.

What feelings are you trying to avoid? What would happen if you just let yourself feel them? Instead of trying to insulate yourself from other people and events in the world, try leaning into your feelings. Feel what it's like to be completely open and vulnerable.

Just beneath our feelings is the Feeler causing them and the Healer healing them. Just beneath the sorrow of human error lies an immense Divine joy that everything melts into. The poet and philosopher Kahlil Gibran wrote, "The deeper that sorrow carves into your being, the more joy you can contain." If you avoid feeling the sorrow, you can't really get to the joy. Only by being completely open and vulnerable to all of life's experience do you discover the power of your own nature.

Our Common Story of Self-Discovery

I'm a real sucker for stories of people who've faced some kind of obstacle or challenge and triumphed over it. I love watching shows on TV about makeovers, where they take some plain-dressed woman and turn her into a goddess, or the shows about people losing weight. I think there's something in the human psyche that draws us to stories of people who thought less of themselves at one point but then came to personal power.

That's what the Bible is. It's a library of books telling the stories of how people found their way to self-discovery and personal triumph. However, I think instead of calling it the Holy Bible, they should have titled it *Sacred Stories*. With that title, perhaps fundamentalists wouldn't be so insistent that every story be taken literally.

The Bible is filled with inspirational stories of triumph over insurmountable odds. It tells what happens when we set an intention for ourselves and try to go forward in life, but still find the past more alluring. The results are: We turn bitter, rigid and then die. That's what happened to Lot's wife when she turned to look back at the city of Sodom. She became a pillar of salt. So the message of the story is: If you want a future better than the past, set your sights on the highest vision you hold for your life, move forward and never look back!

The story of David who faced the huge Goliath with nothing but a slingshot and yet somehow triumphed over him tells us the real power we possess is *inside*. Real strength doesn't come from muscles. It comes from character. We reenact this story in our own lives each time we face a challenge that seems insurmountable, like a frightening medical diagnosis, divorce or long-term unemployment. These things loom like Goliath over us. And yet if we face them with strength and courage, somehow we can make it through.

My favorite Bible story is of Jonah and the whale. Like just about every other main character in the Bible, when God calls on Jonah to fulfill a task, he looks up at the sky and says something like: "Are you high? Dude, you got the wrong person. I am so not ready for that." So when the Old Testament god, Yahweh, tells Jonah to go to the city of Nineveh, he completely ignores him and goes about his own business. In fact, instead of going to Nineveh, where Yahweh told him to go, Jonah boards a ship headed in the opposite direction.

Yahweh doesn't like that. And as we know from other stories about the old god Yahweh, it's not a good idea to piss him off. As the story goes, a storm hits the sea like a bat out of hell. The crew of the ship knows that Yahweh is causing the storm because he's upset with Jonah. So to avoid further wrath, they throw him overboard. He doesn't spend a lot of time on the open seas swimming for his life, however. Jonah is quickly swallowed up by a giant fish. Mysteriously, somehow he survives in the belly of that fish for three days, but you just know it can't smell very good in there.

Now comes my favorite part of the story. Finally, Yahweh takes pity on the disobedient Jonah so he has the fish vomit him up on the beach. Now, there's a friendly gesture from a loving god. I guess the moral of the story is: If you don't listen to what God tells you to do, you end up as whale vomit. What could be worse than that?

Actually, there are a lot of things worse than Jonah's fate. Spending ten or twenty years in a relationship that was never loving is one worse fate. Another is getting up every day forcing yourself to go to a job that you hate. The story of Jonah and the whale tells us what happens when we let our ego get in the way, when we don't listen to that inner voice of Spirit trying to guide us to our highest good.

I can't tell you how many women I've talked to over the years who have told me: "I knew when I was walking down the aisle with the wedding dress on that I was marrying the wrong guy." Like Jonah, we always get into trouble when we don't listen to our heart, that inner guidance that comes directly from God.

Many of the stories we read in books, watch on TV and hear in songs are similar. They're the stories of spiritual beings trying to make it in a world disguised as human bodies. They're the stories of our quest to awaken to the power and potential we hold inside, the stories of our struggle to accept love and show compassion. They're the stories of how we gain self-value and finally have the courage to insist on being treated with respect and honor.

We all have the same story. It is the story of self-discovery. We're just in different chapters. In other words, as a friend of mine who moved to a new city, but took all of the same problems with him, said: "Same drama, different stage!"

Your Story

What's your story? What challenges do you have? What do you struggle with? What Goliath do you face? Was there a time in your life when, like Jonah, your intuition told you to do one thing, but you ignored it and did another? How did that work out for you? Have you ever felt like God vomited you out on a beach? Have you spent too much time looking back at the past, like Lot's wife? Did it free you from the past, or just make you more bitter, like a pillar of salt?

The stories of your life are created and produced by your Higher Self, that part of you that some people call the soul, which is the true essence of who you are. They are not random events. They are not happening by accident. You are not a victim of circumstances. Nobody "up there" is mad at you.

Your stories, whether you label them good or bad, are designed specifically with your spiritual growth in mind. They are part of your awakening. Their purpose is to guide and mold you into the person you are to become. They are supposed to be used to build your character, find your faith and remind you of the truth. They are not supposed to permanently wound or damage you.

The problem is, we take our stories too personally. We get wounded by the circumstances or one of the characters, and as a result get trapped in the story, doomed to repeat it over and over again. When we think of ourselves as victims in the story instead of the producers of a self-created drama, it's easy to fall in the trap of blaming others for our situation or position in life.

My friend and colleague August Gold says, "Everything that happens to you, happens *for* you," reminding us that everything that happens to us in life serves a purpose. That purpose is to awaken you to your power as a spiritual being and call your life into nobler action. Although it may be hard to imagine how cancer, or the loss of someone you love, can be *for* you, nonetheless those events do force us to go down a different path than we would have otherwise taken. And it is on that particular path where our greater good lies in wait for us, just up ahead.

Too many people get trapped in the stories of their lives and forget the only purpose of the story is to find the meaning in it. The story does not have to become a recurring event, repeating itself over and over again. You release yourself from the past and heal it by becoming conscious of the power you hold as the creator of the story, not the victim in it.

Perhaps you were raised in a dysfunctional family. That's part of your story. It contributed to the person you are today. Each member of your family served as a teacher. They were part of your story so you could see an example of what choices people make, and how their lives are affected by those choices. Like it or not, you learned something from them. Whether you label it good or bad, you gained something of value from the experience of growing up in a dysfunctional home, even if it was just to show you the choices you *don't* want to make.

EXERCISE:
SELF-DISCOVERY

Spend some time reflecting on the stories of your life. Which one is the most dramatic? Which one do you hear yourself tell others repeatedly? Which one taught the most powerful lesson? Which one hurt the most? What was the hardest lesson you ever learned? Who was the teacher of that lesson?

Consider making a video recording of you telling your story or answering the questions listed above. When you are finished, watch the recording. How did it feel to watch yourself tell the story? What will be different the next time you tell it?

You Are Part of the Bigger Story

We look too closely at life and judge too quickly. We need perspective, especially when it comes to understanding the stories of our lives. If you stand back, just far enough away from your own personal story, you'll see the big picture, the greater story of humanity. I call that story *Consciousness Awakening*.

We can't pretend there's nothing going on in our world. Something's happening to us, something wonderful.

The psychics predicted it. The mystics can feel it. Scientists theorize about it, and the artists and poets are shouting it from every canvas and performance hall.

The great philosopher William Irwin Thompson said that up until now we've been suffering from some kind of collective hypnosis that's prevented us from seeing who we really are. He said, "We are like flies crawling across the ceiling of the Sistine Chapel. We cannot see what angels and gods lie underneath the threshold of our perceptions." But something's changed, a window has blown open and now we can see those angels and gods. It's as if some kind of evolutionary code has been activated in us and we're all waking up from a long sleep that's kept us blind to the greater story of our lives.

This awakening is happening individually, one person at

a time, but it's also happening collectively to the entire race. The Giant is waking up. The Divine spark within us has been lit. And this is causing us to move out of the survival-oriented species we used to be into a co-creative partnership with Spirit. The purpose of this awakening is for us to fulfill our destiny to create a world that works for everyone, not just a privileged few. It is to awaken us to our connection to every life on the planet.

There is evidence of consciousness awakening everywhere. The most compelling is the appearance of so many visionaries in our world today. Historically, visionaries are the predecessors for creating a new story of how we show up as a people. In the ancient past, very few could actually see our future destiny. The gifted few who would come along every century or two each hinted that we were created for some greater purpose. In one way or another, every spiritual leader and visionary has said the same thing: "Now we are gods. The things I do, you shall do even greater things than these."

In the last few decades, however, visionaries have been coming out of the woodwork. Dr. Martin Luther King Jr. is an example. He came to share his dream of a more just America, one that worked for everyone regardless of their skin color. Many others followed him with their vision of an equal world. Today there are millions more awakening, each sharing a common insight that the day has arrived for us to think and act as one people in one world.

It's our highest potential that scares us the most. That's why, in the past, we always killed the visionaries and messengers of truth. We know how to be *victims*. We know how to play dumb and pretend that what we do doesn't matter. It's the call to greatness that scares the hell out of us. It's the call to conscious action that frightens us the most.

This call to greatness is getting louder and louder. The visionaries have arrived and they are rising up to speak the truth that we have something more to offer the world and each other than just our personal human drama. And their message is scaring people. That's why we're also seeing such a rise in fundamentalism and religious intolerance.

Fundamentalists react to change fearfully. Their message is always the same: We must go back to the way things used to be. They try to put the cork back in the bottle. Their solution is to close us in, build walls and protect borders. But it's too late for that to work. Isolationism won't work in today's world of instant communication and a borderless Internet. So in the end, all of their efforts to hold us back will fail and human consciousness will evolve.

We stand on the shoulders of giants, those generations who went before us to pave the way for our vision. And because we stand on their shoulders, we can see further ahead.

And it's that higher view that's inspiring our awakening. It's happening to all of us right now. We're waking up to our spiritual potential and the power we've always had to change the world. That's the bigger story that we're all a part of: the conscious awakening of planet Earth.

We've finally reached the tipping point in our evolution as a species, that end place that Nature always brings things to right before it transforms them. Biologists say that ten billion seems to be the magic number required before a new level of evolution can emerge. Coincidentally, or perhaps not so coincidentally, it takes about ten billion atoms to make a cell and ten billion cells to make a human brain.

In just a few years, probably in our own lifetime, we'll see the population of our planet reach the ten billion mark. Maybe that's what Nature has been waiting for all along. Maybe that's the tipping point we have to get to in order to transform our crisis into an opportunity and have a new consciousness emerge.

The bigger story of humanity is: Spirit is awakening within us as individuals. Its Power is pushing us out beyond our limitations and small estimations. It is a call to personal greatness. It is a demand on our Divine potential that up until now has mostly been lying dormant within.

That's what your restlessness is about. That's why you often feel as if there's a better way for you to live. Perhaps you're already showing symptoms of the bigger story being activated in your consciousness.

Three Symptoms of Consciousness Awakening

You are changing. Something is happening to you that you can't always explain or understand. And if you're like most people, you're probably not talking about it very much because you're not sure what's happening. There's a new restlessness in your spirit that may be showing up as frustration or anger. You may be experiencing a growing intolerance for injustice and ignorance. Below is a list of three symptoms that many people are experiencing. Perhaps you can relate to them.

SYMPTOM NUMBER ONE

You are experiencing an increased awareness or sensitivity. Suddenly you start having experiences that can't be logically explained, things you don't tell anyone because they'll think you're nuts. There are peak moments and intuitive flashes. In an instant you just know things you've never known before. You become very clear on something you've never even considered before.

You're getting your first taste of what it's like to transcend your ego mind and touch the Mind of God. You're starting to feel your connection to the whole. And from this experience, you start to sense: I am more than this personality that others see. I'm not just a collector of struggles and stories. Your essential self, that deeper, hidden part of you, is being turned on and activated. It's starting to grow and push you out of old opinions and negative thinking.

SYMPTOM NUMBER TWO

As you start to sense your oneness with Spirit, you're probably experiencing a huge surge in creativity. You're waking up with new ideas all of the time; new ways to express yourself in relationships, new concepts for businesses. All kinds of new ideas begin to explode in your mind.

These new ideas that are pouring through your mind are starting to make you uncomfortable. What once was appropriate and acceptable isn't anymore. Now it's not satisfying enough to just make money. Now you want to match *who* you are to what you *do* for a living. You're having a vocational awakening—a call to use the unique talent Spirit placed within you. You are awakening to your destiny, which is to leave the world better than you found it.

You may also be experiencing a sense of urgency. You may be thinking to yourself: "I only have so much time to be who I am and give what I have to give. I've got to get started now!"

SYMPTOM NUMBER THREE

Sometimes this awakening can cause you to feel a sense of being overwhelmed or of regret. So you might be experiencing confusion, frustration or even bouts of depression. That happens because it is the beginning of the end of who you used to be. It's the residual victim-consciousness left over from the *old* you, mourning its own death. If this is happening to you, don't be afraid. Let it have its moment. Honor your feelings and trust that they are a temporary experience in your growth. You will move through this period quickly and get to the other side, where the *new* you is waiting.

We're getting glimpses of the life we're supposed to be living on planet Earth. That's what the great awakening is all about. We can't go back to the life we once lived. We can't pretend we're separate anymore, or that what we do on this side of the planet doesn't affect the people on the other side.

This story that feels so personal to us is really the story of the entire human race. It is the story of our awakening. This is how futurist Barbara Marx Hubbard describes what we're going through: "We are a slowly awakening planetary giant just beginning to realize that we are one living body responsible for its own future in a universe of unknown dimensions."

We are here to create a future more magnificent than we can even imagine and we're just getting started. You are part of the process. You are part of the story. All of the work that you're doing to heal your life and overcome your own personal challenges is not done in vain. It's all part of the bigger story: the story of Spirit waking up in the hearts and minds of its beloved creation.

Now that you've been awakened, the next step to discovering the power of you is to fully and completely accept who you are.

three

Self-Acceptance

I must be myself. I cannot break myself any longer for you, or you. If you can love me for what I am, we shall be the happier. If you cannot, I will still seek to deserve that you should. I will not hide my tastes or aversions. I will so trust that what is deep is holy, that I will do strongly before the sun and moon whatever inly rejoices me and the heart appoints.

—RALPH WALDO EMERSON,
"SELF-RELIANCE"

When I was in sixth grade, my best friend, Ronnie Donoho, and I were inseparable. We did everything together. And because it was 1968 and music was such an important part of our lives, we were totally into the singing group The Monkees. I knew the words to every song they sang and watched every episode of their TV show. We even wore our hair like one of the band members, Peter Tork: strategically dipped below one eye, just long enough to make you jerk your head back and forth every few minutes so you could see from underneath. We thought that was *really* cool.

I wanted to be like my friend Ronnie, so I tried to do everything the way he did. I liked the same music as he did. I wore the same style of clothes. We even had the same kind of bike. After a while we became so much alike it was hard to tell us apart.

Psychologists say when we're young and our own identity isn't yet fully developed, we tend to imitate others. It's all part of the healthy development of our personalities. Since we don't know much about our own tastes and talents yet, we tend to mimic those of our peers. That's why young people are so impressionable and their friends are such an integral part of their lives.

At a young age, we find being accepted by others is very important. So much so, that many of us are willing to sacrifice our own identity just to gain their acceptance. It's not until sometime after puberty that we begin to notice the distinct differences between what we want and what everyone else does. It's the psychological counterpart to the "terrible twos," that age when you discover you have a body and a will separate from your mother. That's why a two-year-old's favorite words are *no* and *mine*. They're just beginning to exercise their own will.

So when we reach those post-pubescent years, sacrificing our own identity to be accepted by others begins to lose its appeal, *if* we're maturing properly. The problem is, many of us don't mature. Our bodies grow up but we get stuck emotionally in that teenage era when we're still trying to find our own identity. The fact is, there are a lot of people walking around out there in the world without a full sense of their own character, willing to do just about anything to be accepted by others, even if it means sacrificing their own integrity.

There are many reasons why some of us don't fully develop into confident individuals. First of all, we live in a culture that rewards conformity. People who are different get ridiculed or shamed until they get back in line with the social norm. Second, many cultures don't have rites of passage for young people, so it's difficult for them to know when it's time to mature and take on their own individuality.

Since conformity is so richly rewarded in our society, it

takes a great deal of courage to be oneself, to stand apart from the crowd and say, "This is who I am, take it or leave it." That kind of courage takes some time and experience to develop. It mostly comes to those who have spent years try- ing to be something they're not, or pretending to be some- thing they thought they should be. Finally the day arrives when they can't stand the pretense any longer and some- thing in them wants to shout to the world, "You will have to accept me as I am, or leave me the hell alone!"

For many people, this personal declaration of indepen- dence doesn't come until later, near midlife. After having spent most of their lives sacrificing their own identity and integrity for others, the day finally arrives when they can't stand it one more minute. Generally speaking this doesn't turn out well. It usually results in some sort of midlife crisis causing people to make decisions out of whim instead of wisdom. That's why fifty-year-old men buy red sports cars and hook up with co-workers, or women decide suddenly one day to leave the family and run off to India. They are in search of themselves. They have settled for too long. The choices they made have created too many limitations in life and so their soul screams, "Get me out of here!"

To avoid this fate, you must fully own yourself. You must come to a place of complete acceptance of everything that makes you who you are. When you stop trying to be like others or to be accepted by them, you are on the road to full ownership of your own true character. When your primary interest is in expressing who you are instead of mimicking someone else, you are on the path to self-acceptance.

An Island of Diversity in a Sea of Sameness

On my route to the grocery store from my home I pass by the offices of a major communications corporation. Outside the building on the corner where I make my turn is a beautifully landscaped area. For the last ten years, the landscaping plan has been exactly the same. Every fall, dozens of perfectly spaced rows of yellow tulip bulbs are planted, all in uniform pattern. And of course each spring, on cue, the yellow tulips bloom. As I drive by, I admire the symmetry of their design. When the wind blows, all of the yellow tulips seem to dance and sway together in perfect unison. It's quite impressive.

However, last year as I drove by, I noticed something different. They were still there; all of the yellow tulips fully bloomed as expected, each one in unison and perfect alignment. But right smack in the middle of all of that yellow was one red tulip, one unplanned, unorganized, unexpected red tulip in a sea of yellow that seemed to shout, "I am here and there's nothing you can do about it."

To the landscaping team, I'm sure it seemed as though a terrible mistake had been made. One red tulip bulb had somehow made its way into the dozens of yellow. However, to Mother Nature no mistake was made. She did it on purpose. That's the nature of Nature, to throw something in the mix of things that doesn't really belong there. But undeniably it's still there.

I wanted to pull my car over and applaud that red tulip. I'm weird that way. I have a great appreciation for diversity, for that one thing that dares to stand out from all of the rest. And I prayed the landscapers wouldn't insist on conformity and pull it out. To their credit, they didn't. For as long as the yellow tulips lasted that spring, one red one remained at the center shouting, "Look at me. I'm different from the rest."

Maybe you know what it feels like to be that red tulip, to be an island of diversity in a sea of sameness. Maybe you're the person who's different from most others around you, the one who feels differently or has a belief system that doesn't match theirs. Maybe you're the weird one in your family or at work. Maybe you're the red tulip! If so, I applaud you. I respect the courage it takes to not try to be like the rest or acquiesce to other people's opinions just to fit in.

Society is in love with conformity. People find comfort in sameness. And yet Nature abhors it. Every creation is unique. Every snowflake has a different design. Every person's DNA is unique. The Creator never repeats itself. We must take our cue from the Creator and learn to respect our differences. They are the only things that makes us interesting.

Nature is funny. Like that one red tulip, she always throws something in that can't be explained away or discounted, something that has to be noticed and dealt with, whether you like it or not! That's why parents who are fundamentalists end up with a gay son, or left-wing, bleeding liberals will have a daughter who is a Republican. That's why New Age parents who schooled their children in the art of crystals, energy healing and all of the other New Agey stuff will have one child who becomes a born-again Christian.

Nature loves to take us off course, to challenge our beliefs, to force us to dig deeper to love people whom we don't understand. She loves to upset our normal, everyday routines and take us out of our comfort zone. That's why she puts things in our path that we think don't belong there. And there are good reasons for the unexpected twists that Nature brings, these unplanned events.

Why Me, God?

If you're like me, you probably don't like to have your schedule changed or plans disrupted. We are truly creatures of habit. I have a friend who eats the same thing for breakfast every day: oatmeal. I know a woman who's worn the same perfume for twenty years. I don't know what she'll do if they stop making it. I drive the same route to work each day. We like our routines and habits. They give us the illusion of control.

But the Creator is unimpressed with our habitual thinking and boring routines. There is no affection in the universe for the mundane. And so even though things appear to happen randomly, the events of our lives are not unscheduled. They show up for a reason. There is a purpose to all of the things that happen, whether we call them good or bad.

Most people get up every day and do the same thing they did the day before and think the same thoughts. We go along pretending one day will be pretty much like the next. Until one morning, you feel a lump in your breast or you come home from work and your spouse says, "I don't love you anymore." And when that happens, we usually ask: "Why did this happen to me?" "Why did I have to get cancer?" "Why did my marriage have to end?" "Why me?"

The answer is: More than likely you've been on the same course for too long. Something had to happen to force you to look at life differently or explore a new path. The challenges we face make us take turns in life that we wouldn't have otherwise taken. They make us explore a different path on our journey. They're kind of like our family members. Think about it—if Nature hadn't thrown your family together with a biological connection, would you have *chosen* to put those people in your life? Some would say not. But now that they're there, you have to learn to love them. You have to find ways to forgive them for things you wouldn't forgive anyone else of.

The unexpected, unplanned and sometimes *unwanted* experiences of your life force you to grow. That's why they come into your life, to take you off course so you'll discover new lands. They come to challenge you to go deeper, to love more unconditionally, to show more compassion and ultimately just to be more. In his essay on compensation, Ralph Waldo Emerson wrote: "Every man in his lifetime needs to thank his faults. . . . Our strength grows out of our weakness. The indignation which arms itself with secret forces does not awaken until we are pricked and stung and sorely assailed."

I bet if you're diagnosed with cancer tomorrow, you're not going to say: "Oh, yippee! Just what I wanted, something new to challenge me." I seriously doubt if you lose your job this week, your first response will be to go home and tell your family: "Oh, goody. Now we get to see how we're going to live on a lot less than we're used to." I don't expect you to be excited or happy that something has come along to challenge your life. But the truth is: You will get through it, and when you come to the other side, you'll be stronger and wiser. And there will be some gift in it, something of value that it brings to your life. The words to the Kelly Clarkson song are true, "What doesn't kill you makes you stronger." And that's because of those "secret forces" Emerson wrote about in his essay, the powers we don't even know we have until some challenge forces us to use them.

If you talk to any cancer survivor, person who is HIV positive, or anyone who's been through a major challenge in life, they'll tell you, "This experience changed my life forever. I had no idea I was so strong." As odd as it may seem, many of them say, "I'm actually grateful this happened to me."

If you are facing a major challenge in your life today, know this: The day will come when you'll look back at whatever you're going through right now and say, "It made me a better man," "I'm a much wiser and stronger woman."

You don't have to be happy when something challenging comes along to take you off course. And I doubt that when it first happens you'll feel very grateful, but remember in the midst of it to stay conscious. Wake up and look around. You're being taken off course for a reason. There's something you're supposed to see that you're not seeing, something of value for you to gain in going through this challenge.

It is specific to your growth. It has been designed especially for you *personally*. Let your strength grow out of your weakness. Call forth those "secret forces" lying dormant within you. Learn what you need to learn. Take what you're supposed to take from it. And if you can do all of that, you'll never have to meet that challenge again.

This is the difference between those who see themselves as powerful co-creators with the Universe, and those who see themselves as victims. When something comes along to challenge them, the spiritually mature say to themselves, "Everything unfolds for my greater good. Somehow, some way, this too will make my life better. I trust God to ignite those secret forces within me to meet this challenge." But those who are immature see themselves as victims, so when something comes along to challenge them they ask, "Why me? Why is this happening to me? What did I do to deserve this?"

Nobody gets through life without facing some major challenge. So, if you haven't had one yet, one is probably on its way to you. Something will happen to veer you off course. There will be some unplanned, unexpected twist to force you off the path you're on. And when it does, remember: You have everything you need to meet the challenge before you. You will emerge on the other side of it triumphantly. Everything that happens *to* you, happens *for* you.

I Will Love You When . . .

The greater lesson in all of this is self-acceptance. It's easy to feel good about yourself when you have money in the bank, someone who loves you and a successful career. The challenge is for you to accept yourself in *any* and *every* condition and to not have your self-worth fluctuate just because circumstances change.

We have too many self-imposed conditions on our own approval. "I'll feel better about myself when I lose ten pounds," we tell ourselves. "I'll be happier when I get a date," we say. Our approval and self-love is too conditional. We're always waiting for another day to be happy or feel good about ourselves.

When it comes to self-acceptance, my dog, Jack, is the best teacher around. He doesn't care what I look like in the morning. He doesn't care how much money I have in the bank or who likes me at work. He doesn't know how old I am. And I can tell he has no interest at all in my grooming rituals because he looks up at me in a peculiar way each morning as I take a shower and blow-dry my hair as if to say, "Why do you go through all of that work just for your appearance?"

Jack also doesn't have any issue with his own self-acceptance. When I take him to the park for a walk, he's not comparing himself to the other dogs. He doesn't lower his head and think, "Oh, if I were only taller like that standard poodle over there by the tree." He seems quite happy being who and what he is. When he sees a cat, he doesn't think, "If only I could learn to meow and prance around a bit more, maybe people would like me better." Jack is a shih tzu and seems pretty happy about it.

What are you waiting for? What are you using as a reason to not accept yourself? How much longer will you wait? How many more years have to pass before you can say, "I love you just as you are right now. I accept you in any and every condition."

Who Told You That You Were Naked?

> The man and his wife heard the sound of Yahweh God walking in the garden in the cool of the day, and they hid from Yahweh God among the trees of the garden. But Yahweh God called to the man. "Where are you," he asked. "I heard the sound of you in the garden," he replied. "I was afraid because I was naked, so I hid." "Who told you that you were naked?" he asked.
>
> —GENESIS 3,
> New Jerusalem Bible

No better question has ever been asked by the god Yahweh in the Old Testament: "Who told you that you were naked?" That's an interesting question coming from a supposedly omniscient, omnipresent, omnipotent God. If God is all-knowing, everywhere present simultaneously throughout the universe and all powerful as the Bible suggests, why would he ask any question at all? God must know the answer to every question.

The story is not a literal account of what happened one day between Adam and God. It is a metaphor, which teaches a powerful lesson of self-acceptance. Adam hid because he was ashamed of his naked body. Before eating of the fruit of the tree of knowledge, Adam felt no shame. He had nothing to hide. He was in right relationship with God. They were best buds, hanging out during the day, just chilling in the garden. But as soon as he became aware of duality (good and evil), he immediately hid himself in shame.

Perhaps Yahweh should have asked a few more questions such as: "Since I made you from my own image, crafted from perfection, what could you possibly find wrong with yourself? If I am the keeper of all knowledge and my wisdom is perfect, why would you listen to another voice, especially one that lies to you? Who told you that you have anything to feel ashamed of? Who told you something was wrong with you? Bring me the liar!"

Many of us have listened to the voice of the liar, the ones who told us we are less than what Spirit created us to be. Maybe it was a teacher who called you stupid, or another kid in school who made fun of you. Maybe it was even a family member who put you down or made you feel ashamed. Whatever the case, they all lied. They didn't see the truth of who you are, the Divine potential you hold inside. They weren't able to see it within themselves, so they couldn't possibly see it in you. You must forgive them for what they didn't know and couldn't see.

The truth is: You are made in the image and likeness of God's wholeness and perfection. And that means inherently there's nothing wrong with you. You have nothing to be ashamed of. And even though you've made mistakes in life, everything you did came from the wisdom you possessed at the time. If you would have known better, you would have done better. We are all operating at peak performance, doing the best we can with the wisdom we have. Knowing this truth will not only help you accept yourself, it will also make it easier to accept others.

Because we live in a world filled with lost souls just trying to find their own way to truth, sometimes self-acceptance can be a real challenge. Very few of the voices we hear tell us the truth. Mostly they are voices of fear and ignorance. Finding your way to self-acceptance through this maze of misinformation and untruths is your soul's greatest achievement.

In an advertisement I once saw on TV for a gym, a man was faced with the choice of whether to go to the gym or eat ice cream. On one shoulder stood an angel saying, "Go to the gym. You'll feel better about yourself." On the other shoulder was a devil who said, "Eat ice cream. It's good. It will make you feel good right now." Of course, he was faced with the challenge of which voice to listen to. And so are you, every day.

Who told you that you were naked? Who told you that you're not good enough? Who told you that you don't have the talent to make your dreams come true? How many people have lied to you? Why do you keep listening to them?

The quality of your life and the state of your mental health is determined by which voice you listen to and entertain in your mind. If you continue to listen to those who question your worth, your inner dialogue will begin to mimic their lies. Before too long, you will question your worth and feel insecure about yourself.

You Shall Know the Truth

Because we all live in a world filled with lies, opinions and untruths, it's important that we take responsibility for what enters our mind and shows up in our lives. It is recorded that Jesus said, "You shall know the truth and the truth shall set you free." Sorting out the lies to uncover the truth of who you are is worth the effort. The rewards are confidence and higher self-esteem. The effect is a life free from self-doubt and insecurity.

Start today by making a different choice. Turn away from thoughts of self-doubt. Refuse to entertain lies in your mind. Replace them with the truth. Here are some affirmative statements that you can use in replacement. Say them aloud each day until you feel the positive shift take place in your self-image. Then write your own.

I am responsible for the quality of my own life because I am in charge of what I think.

My self-worth is determined by the power and presence of God within me, not by the people around me.

I am in charge of my own destiny. I am the captain of my own ship. I choose what enters my mind and my world

My thoughts are centered and focused in the affirmative. I consciously direct them toward that which I want to see manifest in my life.

I do not allow negative thoughts to take up residence in my mind. I am quickly losing interest in their mindless monkey chatter.

I love myself exactly as I am right now. I do not have to lose weight, get more money or find a mate before I approve of who I am.

The Meaning of Life

A couple of years ago I was in the studio doing a webinar that was being broadcast live to a few thousand people. After being on the air for two hours, at the very end of the broadcast the interviewer says, "Dr. Chris, we only have about thirty seconds left, and I just have one more question for you: What's the meaning of life?" And I said, "You want me to answer that in thirty seconds, do you? Well, actually I can."

The meaning of life, and more specifically the purpose of *your* life, is to fully express all that God has created you to be, to not leave this planet with one ounce of potential left inside you. Give the world the full dose. It's just that simple. You are here to be what Nature intended you to be: a fully expressed, once-in-a-lifetime, never-again-repeated-in-all-of-history, unique, strange and powerful individual.

You would think that would be pretty easy to do. If all we have to do is be what Nature intended us to be, you would assume we'd discover that fairly early in life and set out doing it. But it doesn't happen that way. We just don't hear that message very often.

No one told me to boldly go where no man has gone before, except in the opening credits of *Star Trek*. When I was a young boy, no one said, "Trust your heart, Chris. It knows the real you. Don't conform to others' wishes. Find the talent God gave you. It's been left inside awaiting your discovery." Most people don't hear that kind of message, unless they have an enlightened family member who encourages them or a teacher at school who is able to see in them what they don't yet see in themselves.

How do you think the world would be different if we told every child, "Your only duty in life is to be what you are. Be true to your nature. Stay true to your talent. Be yourself." How do you think *your* life would have been different if someone had told you that at five years old, or ten or even twenty?

I guess just about everyone wishes they knew that simple truth long ago. Perhaps it could have saved us from bad marriages, poor choices and wasted time. Nonetheless, since today is the only day we have to live, it makes no sense to live with yesterday's regret. Otherwise you let that regret ruin the opportunities in the present moment.

There's a sequence to our lives; a time to not know the truth, and then a time to know it; a time to hide who we are and pretend we're not worthy, and then a time to stand up and claim our authority. Everybody wakes up in the right sequence and time for their soul's journey. So don't waste time regretting the past. You're here now. You're alive today. You made it through whatever it is you went through and you're still standing.

You are here to find yourself, to discover your own inherent power and purpose. And then once you make that discovery, to let it loose in the world. Being your unedited, uncompromised self will bring all of the meaning to your life.

To Be, or Not to Be

I'm part Native American. My ancestors were born in Oklahoma, long before it was a state. Back then it was simply called Indian Territory. It's where my tribe is from. We are Comanche. Even though I am mostly Caucasian, I can relate to the simple and profound wisdom of Native Americans. A great and wise man from the Lakota tribe known as

Sitting Bull said this: "I am a red man. If the Great Spirit had desired me to be a white man he would have made me so in the first place."

I doubt that Sitting Bull would have been interested in the popular notion of skin bleaching. I don't think he had much desire to dress in a suit like a white man, or in trying to be anything except what the Great Spirit created him to be. He knew who he was: a red man! And he was proud of not just the color of his skin, but the rich heritage of his people. You have to respect that. But more than that, it's also wise to follow his lead, to be what Nature created you to be no matter who opposes it.

Though our society appreciates confident, secure individuals, it makes no accommodation for them. It prefers conformity over individuality. So if you choose to stand out from the crowd and express your uniqueness, don't expect applause. It's highly doubtful many people will celebrate that moment. More than likely just the opposite will occur. You'll probably be ridiculed or ostracized. But fear not, because historically, you're in good company. Galileo was ostracized. Jesus was ridiculed. There was an FBI file on Dr. Martin Luther King Jr.

The voice of mediocrity gets louder and louder, the further you step away from the crowd to follow your own path. Let their fearful chatter be the background noise you train your mind to ignore. Listen closely to the Creator's voice within you and learn to tune out the rest. Let it be the one voice you hear above all others. Train your mind to listen and hear it. Like Sitting Bull, you can trust that the Great Spirit knew what it was doing when it made you who you are.

In his essay on self-reliance, Ralph Waldo Emerson wrote, "My life is not an apology, but a life. It is for itself and not for a spectacle." A recent study showed that women say "I'm sorry" more often than men. Perhaps women apologize more because they're empathetic emotionally and more concerned for another's well-being. Personally, I think it's because women have been socialized to think they have to apologize for just being alive, or for taking up space, or for having the audacity to ask for what they want. If you are a woman, try a little experiment. Write down how many times you apologize in a day. And then become conscious of exactly what you're apologizing for.

Man or woman, your purpose is the same: You are on this earth to live your life in a way that makes you proud, in a way that honors your Divine nature. You are here to be what the Great Spirit created you to be. And that may not please other people. They may not understand your choices. They may not agree with your chosen path. But even then, it's not something you should apologize for.

Stop apologizing for who you are and for what Nature has designed you to be. Your life is not an apology; it's a life. And it will be a life well-lived if you remain true to your authentic self. The answer to the question "To be or not to be?" is *be*!

The Full Dose on the First Date

When I was in my early twenties, I entered the adult dating pool. Little did I know then that a lot of people had gone before me who had been peeing in that pool. And even though most of the time I was shivering down at the shallow end, too afraid to get completely wet, every once in a while I would find somebody I wanted to go out with. Not having a full sense of myself, when I would go out on a date, I would try to be what I thought the other person wanted me to be. Like most people who are afraid to be who they really are, I became convinced I'd be more accepted by others if I could somehow "tone down" the Chris Michaels's version.

That was my strategy: to tone down, to be less exuberant and enthusiastic. I did that because my friends at the time and most of the people I had already gone out with said, "Chris, you are just too much! You're too conscious. You're too awake. You have too many expectations. And most people can't handle that." So I thought, okay, I can tone it down a bit. I can try to be less enthusiastic. But then it occurred to me that I have no clue how to be *less* than what I already am. Should I pretend to be less wise? How do you practice being unconscious? How can you put yourself back to sleep once you've had an awakening?

Needless to say, my strategy failed. I just didn't know how to tone myself down. Plus, I figured that eventually if I kept dating someone, at some point they're going to see the real me anyway. So why not show them what that is up front? Why not give them the full dose on the first date?

Then it occurred to me that maybe my friends were right, maybe I am too much for *most* people. But this is how Nature designed me, so the person who would be attracted to me is going to be looking for someone courageous and conscious. They're not going to be like *most* people. They're going to have to be extraordinary. And it wasn't long after that when I met my partner, whom I've been with for almost twenty years.

The moral of the story is: Whatever you are by nature, keep to it. Never desert yourself or the unique way God created you to express. Be what Nature intended you to be. Be true to your own heart. Follow your own inner guidance. It will lead to your true destiny, a destiny that will fulfill your greatest dreams and wildest imagination. Give the world the full dose on the first date.

Three Truths to Guide You on the Road to Self-Acceptance

TRUTH NUMBER ONE: You Are Not Here to Learn. You Are Here to *Live*.

Though it's wildly popular in New Age circles, as well as fundamentalist religions, to believe that we are all *children* of God, the Creator is not a parent. The Power that creates and sustains an infinitely expanding universe is not into the daily drudgery and sacrifices of human parenting.

I know teachers who are overwhelmed when more than twenty children are in their classroom. Can you imagine being responsible to parent and teach billions of Earth children each day? What a horrible job! And this is just one planet in a vast universe. What if there are trillions of other species all needing education? Talk about a nightmare. And yet many people believe that life is a school and their purpose is to learn lessons, supposedly delivered from on high.

I don't think Spirit is into spending an eternity teaching lessons to unruly, uneducated humans. That can't be any part of a perfect or Divine plan. God is not in the education business. It's in the *expression* business. Like every artist, Spirit creates to express itself. As a perfect Intelligence, it has ideas it wants to manifest. As the Source of beauty, its desire is to create things that are beautiful. As pure and perfect Joy, it wants to take pleasure in creating. As the universe's only perfect Lover, God creates only what it loves.

While it's true that through trial and error you do learn lessons, that's not the primary purpose of your life. Learning is an *effect* of self-discovery. It is not the cause of life. Simply by being alive and making choices every day, you learn which ones bring you in alignment with the nature of Spirit, which is peace, love and joy, and which ones take you in the opposite direction. Your experiences in life are created from your own choices, not a distant deity with a lesson plan.

Since your experience is created by your own individual belief system, however, if you believe life is about learning lessons, guess what's going to happen? Your life will be one lesson after another. Your belief will create a self-fulfilling prophecy carried out each day in the school of hard knocks.

You are not here to learn. You are here to live. You are in this life because Spirit had a new way in which it wanted to express. And so out of itself, in its own image and likeness, it created you as an outlet for that expression and then set you free to discover yourself.

You are not a *child* of God. You are an *expression* of God.

You were created so Spirit could love in the unique way that only you can love. It wanted to see through your eyes, out into the world with the unique perspective that only you hold. It wanted to *be* you and so it created you as a means for its own individual expression.

When you live from this truth, life becomes a journey of self-discovery and acceptance instead of a hardship to endure. Every day is an adventure. Like a small child, you wake up enthusiastic and ready for the new, instead of dreading what horrible lesson you may have to learn that day.

It is written that we must become as *little children* to enter the kingdom of heaven. Heaven is not a faraway location, just beyond the stars. It is a state of consciousness, an awareness of the highest possible good. That's what heaven is. It is the most magnificent thing you can imagine.

Like our image of God, our concept of heaven was also created by primitive man. The people who first imagined it and wrote about heaven were desperately poor. It's no wonder the highest possible good they could imagine was an ostentatious display of earthly wealth with streets paved with gold.

But heaven is something much more than just material wealth. It is an awareness of total peace, unconditional love and complete joy. To gain this awareness and to enter the kingdom of heaven, you must restore and recapture a sense of adventure and joy. You must see life through the eyes of a child, approaching each day with daring and courage.

Stop learning lessons. Stop trying to endure hardship. Stop suffering. It serves no purpose and brings no value to your life. Live your life to the fullest. Approach the new day with a daring sense of adventure. Accept yourself as you are. You are made in the image and likeness of God, so that's got to be good.

TRUTH NUMBER TWO: You Are Not Here to Evolve. You Are Here to *Unfold*.

Most people in the world gained their first exposure to the concept of evolution in the ninteenth century through the work of Charles Darwin. He was the first to formulate a scientific theory on the subject. This theory is widely accepted by educated people today and is deeply ingrained in our culture.

The dictionary defines *evolution* as a process of gradual, progressive change or development. To evolve means to have started as one thing and end up as another. If we started as apes and ended up as humans, then you could say we *evolved* into a new species.

Many people believe that we are here to continue our evolution as a species with hopes that one day we will evolve beyond our current form into another. But I'm not convinced that is our purpose. In fact, I don't believe we're here to evolve at all. I believe we're here to *unfold*. And though it may seem to be a very fine line between the two, they're actually quite different.

When something evolves, it changes into something it's never been before. It becomes something new by taking on additional features and attributes. That's why I don't believe we are evolving. We are not becoming something else. We are unfolding what we've always been.

Everything you're going to be is already contained within you. You are whole and complete, just as Spirit created you. Your mind is equipped to accept new ideas. Your spirit has enough determination to manifest those ideas into reality. Whatever power you think you're going to have someday, you already have. Whatever you're going to be one day, you already are. You just have to unfold it.

To think of yourself as evolving is to see yourself as incomplete. It means that you have to add something you don't yet possess in order to be complete. However, to see yourself as unfolding is to begin with the premise that you already possess everything you need in order to be fulfilled.

You are not evolving. You are unfolding. As you are, right now, you are complete and whole. To succeed in life, you don't need anything other than what you currently possess. You have what it takes to fulfill your dreams. You have access through your thinking mind to the one Mind of the universe, which delivers to you new ideas every day. Your success in life will come from using what you've got right now, not by waiting for something else to be added later.

TRUTH NUMBER THREE: You Are Not Here to *Get* the Best. You Are Here to *Give* the Best.

Because we think of ourselves as needing something other than what we've got to succeed, many people approach life from a *getting* perspective. They believe life will be complete when they get a better job, make more money, or find someone to love. So they go out into the world trying to get outer conditions and circumstances to change. They try to manipulate events or set strategies they hope will get them what they want.

When you know you already have everything you need to succeed contained within yourself, your approach to life is vastly different. Instead of trying to *get* the best, you are trying to *give* the best. Instead of looking for someone out there in the world to get love from, you want to give all of the love in your own heart. Instead of trying to get on some company's payroll so you can get money, you are looking for an opportunity to give your unique talent.

Because you already have enough love in your own heart and enough wisdom in your own mind, your approach to life should always be to find new opportunities to give what you have to the world, not get something from it. Besides, Nature won't allow you to receive something you're not first willing to give. She's smart that way.

How Much Are You Worth?

I was not raised by parents with high self-esteem. Many people aren't. My parents didn't know much about self-worth. They did the best they could in raising their children. But having residual self-doubt that lingered from their own childhood, they were unable to provide an example of high self-worth.

Even though most parents love their children and try to encourage their self-esteem, much of our assessment of our own value comes from the culture we live in, or from the opinions of people around us. And our acceptance of that input is mostly unconscious. Few people have consciously constructed their self-image through careful study and examination. Most have assigned their worth based on unconsciously accepted ideas from the past.

I remember my seventh grade gym teacher, Mr. Nichols, making a derogatory comment about my body that affected my self-image for decades. It took me years to realize that he was just regurgitating his own insecurities and poor body image. It's just these kind of unconsciously accepted lies that destroy our self-image and sabotage our self-worth.

To some degree, we are all victims of victims. Because many of us come from generations of people who struggled to understand their value, we have inherited their confusion. Because we grew up in a world full of people unaware of their worth, it is commonplace to be infected by their disease of low self-esteem. And it's this background that lands many people on a teeter-totter of self-acceptance and self-denial; one that lifts way up in the air when things are going well, but then lands with a hard thump on the ground when conditions change.

The teeter-totter of self-worth leaves people's self-image intact when they have lots of money and things are going well at work and home. They're riding high when they drive an expensive car or live in a distinguished neighborhood. But when the weight of conditions shift to the negative, such as a job layoff or divorce, their self-esteem abruptly hits bottom and the ride on the teeter-totter suddenly isn't fun anymore. Unfortunately, many people know this up-and-down ride all too well. Some people spend their entire lives riding the teeter-totter, with their self-esteem bouncing up and down.

For most of us, self-acceptance is conditional. We approve of ourselves when we lose weight, or finally find a decent relationship. Then, and only then, will we be all right. And until that day comes, we withhold our love and acceptance. There are dozens of conditions that must be met before we find ourselves worthy. Of course, this kind of conditional love keeps our self-esteem from ever rising. It's like running a race with a finish line that keeps moving ahead. You can never make it to the end. You're never going to be good enough!

The only way off the teeter-totter of self-acceptance is to gain a true perspective of who you are, one not based on other people's opinions or the world's infections. You have to begin to see yourself as a spiritual being, not just a human body with a history of experiences. Your self-worth must be anchored in something more solid than the shifting sands of daily human life or past achievements or failures. Your value must be grounded in something permanent and lasting, so you will be able to weather the storms of everyday life. This brings to mind the questions that must be answered so you can determine your true worth:

- Am I valuable because I have a job or make a living?

- Does my worth depend on body type or size?

- Am I worth more when I am in a relationship than when I am not?

- Is my value based on income, assets or position?

- When other people like me and approve of my choices, does that make me worth more?

- Should my self-esteem be higher when I'm feeling happy and lower when sad?

- Do other people's opinions determine my worth?

- Does my own opinion determine my value?

When you can answer *no* to all of these questions, you have come to the end of the teeter-totter ride. Never again will your self-esteem spike and fall. Never again will it be based on outer conditions. You will have found the truth that all confident people stand on, the truth that will forever set you free of self-doubt and the mindless negative chatter that so many people endure each day.

You are valuable to life because of *who you are*, not *what you have done*. Your true worth has nothing to do with personal success or failure. It is not a variable that shifts with conditions. It is a permanently established truth that remains constant no matter what happens to you. It is not determined by other people's opinions or what conditions are current in your life. Even your own opinion of your worth isn't valid. Your value was determined by the Creator on the day you came to life.

Your true worth is as much a part of you as your DNA. It is deeply rooted in the essence of your being. It's as unique as your fingerprint and as eternal as your spirit. Your value comes from the Presence of God that lives in, as and through you, in the once-in-a-lifetime pattern it has created as an outlet for its own expression.

You are much more than the body you occupy or the conditions you survive. You are the life of God making an entrance into the world as an individual spirit. When you identify yourself with that truth, you will never again question your self-esteem. The struggle to accept yourself as you are will be over and a personal freedom will enter your mind in a way you have never known before.

Stop determining your worth by the reflection in the mirror. Give up your own judgments and negative opinions about choices you *should* have made, but didn't. Let go of the guilt and shame that others tried to impose upon you. Release the programming that has you beating yourself up every day with negative self-talk. Stop it!

Underneath the scrap heap of judgment, opinions and unforgiving thoughts is where you will find your true self. Deep inside is the purity and innocence that you came into life with. There was a day when you had no negative self-opinion or body issues to resolve. No baby is lying in the cradle thinking, "Oh, if I could just get rid of these rolls of fat, then I would be worth something." There was a time in your life when you knew your value and never questioned it. Now it's time to get back to that knowing so you can remember who you are.

My dog, Jack, knows who he is. He has no self-esteem issues. And that's because, like all animals, he operates from instinct alone. His mind is not conscious of choice, so he *has* to be exactly what God created him to be. You, on the other hand, are not so lucky. Because your Creator designed you for its fullest expression, it has given you a conscious mind, aware of choice. You can choose to be what God has created and know your worth, or deny it. You have to make this choice every day. Here are a couple of things to consider as you do:

1. **Your mind is your greatest asset, and how you use it determines the quality of your life.**

    You are valuable because you have imagination: the ability to envision life differently than you are living it. Never underestimate the power of this capability. The power of vision is what allowed us to build spaceships that travel to distant planets. It is the source of dreams and dreams fulfilled. Every great invention or piece of art comes from this innate power.

Because we are the only species·on the planet that possesses this grand power of imagination, we have dominion over the rest and a preordained right to choose our own path in life. This power resides within everyone. No matter who you are, or what you have been through, you can still dream. You can still imagine life better. And that is the first step toward making it better.

2. **You are a once-in-a-lifetime opportunity for God to be the unique person it has created you to be.**

There's never going to be another you, ever! God made just one. Nobody talks like you. Nobody thinks as you do. No one can love the way you can love. You're an *original* piece of work, created by a Master Artist. Just think about how valuable that makes you.

Hanging in the Louvre in Paris, France, is the original masterpiece called the *Mona Lisa*, painted by Leonardo da Vinci. His genius makes its way onto the canvas in a style and manner that has been evaluated and analyzed by art historians and critics for centuries. But still the question remains: What is it worth? What value does the painting hold? Since there will never be another one, what is the *Mona Lisa* worth—

$1 million, $10 million, $100 million? Obviously, the painting is priceless.

Now the question that remains is: How much are *you* worth? There's never going to be another one of you. If the *Mona Lisa* is priceless, so are you. After all, you were created and designed by the Genius that inspired Leonardo da Vinci to paint.

Start to anchor your value in who you are by what uniqueness God has placed inside of you. Remember: There's never going to be another chance to be all that you are. This is your opportunity to stand tall, be proud, speak your mind and give your love to the world. It's time to stop questioning your worth and accept the truth that you are priceless.

The Power of Authenticity

My favorite black T-shirt got ruined in the wash the other day, so I went in search of a new one at the mall. This isn't the kind of T-shirt you wear to mow the lawn, it's more dressy, like the ones Simon Cowell used to wear on *American Idol*. The mall near my house is very upscale, filled with high-class stores such as Saks and Neiman Marcus. Given the variety of stores, I never expected my search to be such a difficult task. But apparently there are many different choices for a simple black T-shirt, all of which seem to be assembled in the same country, India.

As I entered the men's department at Neiman's, I was immediately approached by an enthusiastic salesperson. She sent me to the designer rack, where I found a slew of black T-shirts. I couldn't decide between the Dolce & Gabbana or the Armani. So, I turned the sales tag over to compare prices. To my shock and dismay, they were both over two hundred dollars. Needless to say, that was the turning point in the decision-making process. I immediately left the store and went to The Gap, where I bought one for fourteen dollars.

Who in their right mind would pay that kind of price for a black T-shirt? I can see the difference between a designer suit and one off the rack, but a simple, black T-shirt? Come on! And yet, I'm sure they sell. Someone is buying them, or else they wouldn't be manufactured.

I know people who are into labels. They compare notes at parties. I hear them talk about the differences between Prada and Kenneth Cole. They wouldn't dare leave the house without some designer label screaming its name at you on the street.

Don't get me wrong. I love fine clothing and nice things. And I've been known to pay the price for them. What I don't like are pretentious people. I used to *hate* them, but now I have a clearer understanding of where they are coming from.

People who hide behind labels, pretending to be something they're not, do so because they don't believe who they are is good enough. Pretentiousness comes from insecurity. It is a need to prove you are worthy, when in your heart you don't really believe you are. That is not to say that everyone who wears designer clothes is pretentious. They are not. There is a vast difference between wanting something because it is beautiful and needing it because you don't feel complete without it.

In the '70s disco song, Cheryl Lynn sang, "To be real, I've got to be real." Nothing works better than being your true self. There is great power in authenticity. Pretending to be something else weakens you. It delays your fullest expression. It castrates your uniqueness and invalidates your character. To deny your true self is to deny your Creator. Pretending to be something you're not is like saying to God, "I don't trust that what you placed inside of me is good enough."

Inevitably the truth gets told and who you *really* are gets out. You can hide your insecurities only to some. Fools won't be able to tell the difference, but the wise will always see through your pretense.

I had my friend John over for dinner one night and invited him to bring a guest. We all had a good time and enjoyed one another's company, or so I assumed. The next day, I called John to ask if his guest enjoyed the evening. He said, "No, not really." So, I asked why. And he replied, "My friend told me he was uncomfortable because he felt like you could see into his soul." And I said, "Well, he's right. I can see into his soul. And if he wasn't trying to hide something, he wouldn't be uncomfortable." Later I heard John's friend was addicted to drugs and ended up near death in the hospital. I reached out to him with support, even though my presence at the dinner party made him feel uneasy.

Nothing can remain hidden forever. Eventually every truth gets told and every liar exposed. That's why it's important to not delay the inevitable. Be yourself, even if you have insecurities. Expose them for what they are: hidden lies that are fed by the "monkey chatter" in your mind that keeps repeating "You are not good enough" on a loop. Let them come out from underneath the heap of denial where they have been hiding. Show them in the light of day so they may be healed by perfect knowing.

Find the courage to show the world who you *really* are and trust that it is good enough. Surely God has not gone to all the trouble to create you as you are, for you to hide yourself.

Hold steady to the course that leads to the fullest expression of your true self. Don't hide what Spirit has created in you.

Certainly, there are attributes of your character and personality of which you approve and are proud to display to the world, and others which you are not so proud to have. This is true of all of us. We are a collage of contradictions. That's the way it has always been. That is the destiny of a perfect spiritual being, assigned to a flawed human life. We have not been designed by Nature for consistency. The key is to accept yourself in spite of your human flaws.

The truly authentic person is not delusional. They don't just see the good in themselves and deny the bad. They accept it all. Being truly authentic means expressing your full self, not just a portion. Of course, that doesn't mean you should run rampant with those attributes of your character that are not so kind. Every day is a balance between your Divinity and humanity. Work to express more of the former and you will find the latter giving way.

The power of a truly authentic person is genuine. It comes from the freedom of self-expression. An authentic person has no pretense. They have diligently worked to overcome inner doubt and fear. They stand on an authority known only to a few; an authority that inspires the rest of us to let go of our fears and be the original person God created us to be.

In a world that dearly loves conformity, it is empowering to be the one truly unique individual who has left the pack behind. Be that one. Break away from the crowd. Stop giving voice to your fears and insecurities. Stand on your own authority and have the courage to be your true self. If you follow your own unique path, greatness will follow.

The Courage of Nonconformity

A few years ago, I had a speaking engagement in Nashville, Tennessee. Since the host of the event offered to chauffer me around, I chose not to rent a car. Later in the day, I would regret that decision. After being dropped off at my hotel in the evening, I realized the only place to eat close by was a chain restaurant known for "country cookin," which basically means everything is fried.

The hostess seated me all the way in the back of the restaurant. After walking through the entire place to get to my table, and taking a close look at the patrons, it was obvious that I was in the Deep South. I was definitely overdressed. The most represented dinner attire at the restaurant that evening was a pair of overalls. The place was filled with what some people might derogatorily call "rednecks."

As I sat alone, feeling guilty for ordering country-fried

steak and mashed potatoes, I looked up to see a new customer being escorted to a table by the hostess. Everyone in the whole place was watching him and whispering to one another. You could feel the tension in the room.

He walked in with the grace of a gazelle. He strutted his effeminate walk like a supermodel on a runway. Trailing behind him, whirling in the breeze, was a much-too-colorful scarf. Tucked under his arm was a *Vogue* magazine. He was over fifty, with eyebrows arched way too high for a man. It was obvious he had on makeup and eyeliner. He was clearly out of place!

I continued to watch the reaction of the crowd. They were astounded that this flamboyant man could invade their territory. You could see the condemnation on their faces. The air was thick with judgment. They whispered and pointed their fingers.

I watched as he bravely, and *slowly*, made his way to a table. As he sat alone, flipping through the pages of his fashion magazine, I wondered what he must face every day to be so different. How much ridicule does he endure just to be himself? What kind of courage must it take for him to live in a society that would feel much more comfortable if he would dress and act as they do? I decided that I wanted to reward that courage in some small way. So, I called the waitress over and paid his check anonymously.

From the day you were born, someone in your life has tried to get you to conform. "Why aren't you more like your brother?" they ask. "Why can't you be more like your sister?" "I don't understand how you can be the way you are," they bellow. Even though each of us has a completely different appearance, personality and character, some people seem bewildered by the fact that we don't all think and act alike. It's remarkable to them that we don't want exactly the same things they do.

Even though you were born in a country that was founded on individual freedom of expression, you live in a society that does not encourage that behavior. The pressure to conform to the behavior of people around you is intense, and it begins at a very early age. The indoctrination starts in elementary school. By third or fourth grade, you have already learned the price you have to pay for being different. The emotional sting of shame and humiliation is felt early as you quickly learn it is best to get in line with others and avoid being ridiculed.

This unconscious programming continues each day as you move through the awkward years of youth into a fully indoctrinated adult. Before you know it, or have much time to think about it, you are walking, talking and thinking just like everyone else. A quick drive through the suburb of any American city will reveal the pressure to conform. Most houses are painted beige or gray. In some places, the neighborhood association dictates conformity to only one or two color choices.

And yet, the soul cries out for freedom. Deep within is your *true*, authentic self, slowly being crushed under the weight of conformity. Day by day, as you continue to accept the same things others do, a little bit of you withers. If this continues year after year, a sudden panic will occur at midlife, as you discover the life you've been living has never been your own. Questions will arise: "When did I choose this career? Why am I doing this? What do I *really* want from life? Who am I?"

It's been said that slowly we live, and slowly we die. By accepting less than what you truly want, little by little, each day, you find yourself in a life that doesn't match who you really are. In small portions, you have given yourself away, until the day comes when there's nothing left to give.

This destiny can be avoided, but only by those with great courage. It takes a brave soul to resist the temptation of the crowd and the approval of others. We all know what happens when you step away from the crowd and say to the world: "I am going to live by my own rules and be guided by my own heart. I can't live just to make *you* happy. I have to find my own happiness."

As soon as you announce your independence, the war begins. To your surprise, people who you thought would be on your side, rally against you. Even they can't resist the pressure to conform. If *you* step out of line and follow the beat of your own drum, where does that leave them? They will have to face their own acceptance of the status quo, and that's something they are ill prepared to do. So it should come as no surprise they would not support your independent path. Bless them and follow your path courageously. Leave them to their own regrets. Perhaps the day may come when they understand your choice.

To be a nonconformist doesn't mean you are a rebel. You are not rebelling against society. Teenagers rebel. They are fighting the system and resisting authority. You are following your own independent path, one that was chosen specifically to match your unique talent and character. Not conforming to the majority doesn't mean fighting others or putting them down, just to lift yourself up. It is a mark of spiritual maturity to claim your own authority, to trust more in what God has placed inside of you than any external authority. It doesn't mean you are disrespectful of others. It means you respect your own authority first.

Step away from the crowd. Listen to the Spirit within that whispers in your ear, "Follow me. I will take you to your dreams." Be brave. Take bold action toward your best ideas. Let go of the need for others' approval. Feel the strength that comes from insisting upon your own path.

It's time to accept yourself just as you were made. There can be no pretending anymore. You have something to do in the world, something that will make a difference. Now that you've resolved your questions of value, it's time to learn how to use the greatest power known to man.

four

Your Mind and
How to Use It

Whether you know it or not, you have at your command the greatest power known to man. It is your mind, and how you choose to use it determines everything in your life. Even though many of the world's greatest teachers and spiritual masters have told us so, most people are completely unaware that their thoughts have creative power. They listen to the monkey chatter going on inside their heads not knowing their thoughts group together to form beliefs, which then cause their experience.

Of course we all know that every single thought does not itself create. If that were the case, people would be dropping like flies. Their heads would suddenly explode because of one passing thought you had while driving on the freeway.

Who hasn't fantasized about their boss suddenly keeling over, or their children running off with the circus? We all have thoughts racing through our minds that we don't really want to see manifest. That's why the Intelligence that designed our minds created a safety mechanism that prevents that from happening. So, it's not every single thought that is creative, it's your *tendency* of thought that forms the belief system that causes your reality.

Have you ever met someone you instantly like, or had the opposite experience—met someone you don't like at all? Have you ever spent time with someone and left feeling completely drained of energy? It's like they were some kind of emotional vampire that sucked the life out of you. And all you want to do is get away from them as soon as possible. Some people have the opposite effect on us as well. Being around them is such a joy that we don't want to separate. There is a reason for this experience. Every person has a mental atmosphere surrounding them reflecting their tendency of thought. This atmosphere is not visible to the naked eye but is sensed by our own feeling nature. It's what attracts us to some people and makes us want to get away from others.

We reveal our character to the people around us through this mental atmosphere. When we come within range of others, we send out vibes, energy or whatever you want to call it. Much of what we learn about each other comes from this exchange of nonverbal communication. That's why it's difficult to explain in words why you are attracted to some people and not to others. It's just an intuitive thing.

The best way to truly know someone is not to listen to what they say, but to watch everything they do. Our truth is revealed in our *actions*, not in our words. American poet and essayist Ralph Waldo Emerson said it this way: "Who you are speaks so loudly I can't hear what you're saying." Who you are comes from what you think. Thoughts that you choose to entertain on a regular basis become the mental atmosphere surrounding you. That atmosphere dictates your actions and causes your experience. To put it simply, you are what you think, and you attract what you are.

Professional athletes and successful businesspeople know this. They focus their thoughts on what they want to accomplish. They envision success. They repeat affirmative statements. They train their minds to believe in achievement. They use the power of their thoughts to get the results they seek. You can do it too. Just like building muscles in your body, it will take some time and discipline to train your mind, but the results will far outweigh the effort. Make it your goal to think about what you want, and want what you think about.

Like a fish in water, your mental atmosphere is surrounded by Power. This Power is the energy of Spirit and the creative element of the universe. Like the soil, it takes whatever is planted and makes something out of it. So, whatever you are thinking about is like a seed planted in the ground. The Power of Spirit automatically and immediately goes to work drawing into your life the people, events and circumstances that exactly match your thought. This is how it is done unto you as you believe. This is an example of the spiritual law that Moses said is both a blessing and a curse. It is a blessing to those who know how to use it and a curse to those who don't.

A good question that many people ask is: If my thought is creating my experience, why does my life look the same today as it did yesterday? The obvious answer is: Because you keep thinking the same thing. Some studies show that nearly sixty thousand new thoughts enter our minds on a daily basis. But even though you are presented with new ideas each day, the thoughts you choose to entertain on a regular basis have become your habit. And habits are not easily broken.

Your mind has already received training. You have inherited the thoughts of others. Your family of origin became your model for thinking a certain way. If you grew up in a family where people were positive and saw the glass half full instead of half empty, odds are you think that way as well. But if you grew up in a family of fearful, negative people, you may have been infected by their bad attitude. Either way, your thought has received some kind of programming from your childhood experience.

Unfortunately, very few people spend much time reflecting on their thoughts and what ideas they habitually entertain. As they become adults, they just repeat what they learned as children. Not many take the time to closely examine whether what they've been told is even true. They just accept the thought pattern of others and repeat them on a loop, creating the same experience year after year. This is how prejudices pass from one generation to another and why victims of childhood violence become abusers of their own children. What we see and learn from our upbringing gets imprinted on our own mind and repeated in our experience. And of course, all of this takes place unconsciously.

The average person is unaware of the transformative power at their disposal. They don't know that simply by changing the way they think, by establishing a new pattern of thought, they can create an entirely new way of living. By breaking the pattern of unconscious thinking, you can transform your life. By consciously selecting and choosing which thoughts to think and ideas to entertain in your mind, you can heal your body, attract a new love and increase the flow of money into your life. A whole new world of opportunities will open up for you. A host of new creative ideas awaits your discovery.

You are not average. You are not supposed to be living an average life, unconsciously repeating negative patterns. You are an extraordinary being created and sustained by an unlimited Power. The universe did not go to all of the effort to organize your particular DNA, assemble your unique personality and breathe life into your soul, for you to be dull and ordinary. It's time for you to awaken to the power of your mind and learn how to use it to create the life you dream is possible.

The Inner Critic

Do you hear voices in your head? Does one of them say nasty things? Does it constantly judge others and predict the worst possible outcome for every situation? If so, you are living with the Inner Critic. It's easy to recognize his/her voice. She says things like: "Who are you kidding? You could never have *that* guy. He's way out of your league." The Inner Critic says: "Dude, seriously. Do you really think they're going to hire *you*? You know you don't have the skills to do that job."

Even when things are going great in your life, when your

job is secure, someone loves you and you have money in the bank, the Inner Critic says: "It won't last. He's going to leave you. You're going to lose this job. And by the way, have you looked in the mirror lately? It's not good. You're really starting to show your age." On the road to enlightenment, at some point we all have to face and deal with the Inner Critic. We have to find a way to live with that inner voice that never seems to shut up!

Many years ago, when I was first introduced to the concept that my thought had the power to create my experience, I set out to gain control of my thinking. At first this seemed like a daunting task. When I started to pay attention to some of the thoughts that were going through my mind on a daily basis, I was horrified. There was so much negativity and fearful, mindless chatter. Every day, that voice inside my head had some new fearful prediction or negative drama to introduce. And I had no clue how to stop it. Sometimes the voice would get so loud, I would go into the bathroom, look myself in the mirror, and say, "Would you please just shut the hell up?"

As I tried to gain control of my thinking, I wondered, where did all of this negativity come from? When did the Inner Critic's voice take over my mind? And how can I get rid of it? In time, I realized that I was separate from that voice, that it wasn't me. It was the voice of a thousand generations who had gone before me and lived on this planet. It is what's called in metaphysical circles the voice of *race consciousness*.

Even though every person's DNA is different, our bodies are all made from the same basic genetic material. And even though your thoughts are individual, you may hear the echo of the fearful, negative thinking of the entire race in your mind. Like that annoying beeping sound commercial trucks make when they're backing up, let the voice of race consciousness be the background noise you train your mind to ignore. Begin separating your own voice from its fearful predictions and self-defeating drama.

There is another voice inside your mind. It is the voice of Spirit. It is your true, authentic self, not the little ego self, but the Higher Self, which is your individualized God-identity. That voice says things like, "You can accomplish anything you set your mind to do. You are beautiful. Follow me to your true destiny. I love you and will never lead you astray." That voice is fearless. It always speaks of your power and potential. It will urge you to follow your best ideas and have faith in your good.

The voice of faith or the voice of fear: those are your choices. You can give your attention to the Inner Critic or follow the voice of Spirit. Whichever one you choose will determine everything else in your life. That one choice decides whether you'll be happy or not. It decides your health and whether or not you'll find love. It determines if you attract new opportunities in life, or repel them. Every day you have a choice and each new day you have to decide again.

The Inner Critic will never go away or be completely silenced in your mind. It will always be with you trying to convince you to lower your standards and expect less from life. You must learn to live with this obnoxious inner roommate. Just be sure it gets the smallest room in your mind's house. It does not deserve the master suite. A tiny little closet is enough room.

A Twelve-Foot-High, Electrified Barbed-Wire Fence

The fearful, nasty thoughts of the Inner Critic aren't the only thing you have to deal with if you're going to learn to use your mind in a way that creates a powerful, dynamic life. There's no harm caused by any passing thought or idea. The thoughts in your mind are similar to the people you invite into your home. Visitors come for a short stay and then go. It's the people you live with every day that create the quality of your life. That's true of your thoughts as well. The ones you entertain on a daily basis are causative to your experience.

If you have an established pattern of thinking well of

yourself and others on the inside of your mind, you'll display loving qualities on the outside of life. People will automatically be attracted to you. They will enjoy your company. But just the opposite is true as well. If you have an established pattern of angry and resentful thoughts, you will repel good people and have difficulty maintaining healthy relationships. The thoughts you nurture with your time and attention become the dominant state of your mind.

Sometimes certain negative thoughts can get lodged in our minds. Before we have time to notice, thoughts of resentment can begin to clog the natural flow of creativity. Once this happens, the whole system becomes constipated and future good is prevented from entering our lives. If left unattended, thoughts of resentment begin to fester and rot. They will infect every good opportunity and ruin your relationships. Anyone who's been out on a first date with someone new and had to sit across the dinner table listening to them say horrible things about their ex knows what a turnoff that can be. Rarely ever do they make it to the second date.

Resentment is like a twelve-foot-high, electrified barbedwire fence you put around yourself. You built it for good reasons. You've been hurt, abused or treated poorly, so you want to guard yourself. You've been a victim of some great injustice. There are many good reasons for you to be angry or to feel resentment. So to prevent your history from re-peating itself, you build a fence. Next time, if anyone tries to hurt you they'll get zapped, electrocuted and burned.

There are a couple of problems with this strategy, how-ever. First of all, because the fence is so high, no one can climb over it. You are trapped behind it. And in time, that becomes a very lonely place to be. Second, every good thing you dream of having in your life is on the other side of that fence. The love of your life is there waiting for you. A check for a hundred thousand dollars is there written in your name, with a note that says, "Use this money to make your dreams come true." The solution to your problems, the healing of your body is there, just on the other side of the fence. But none of it can get to you.

Here's the ironic truth: The resentments you hold in your mind for others do nothing to hurt them. They block the flow of good into *your* life. They keep good things from you and good people from entering your life. They prevent new opportunities from coming your way. Nothing good can get to you until you tear down the fence.

In 1987, President Ronald Reagan stood at the Branden-burg Gate near the Berlin wall that separated east from west and had the audacity to proclaim, "Mr. Gorbachev, tear down this wall!" What followed was a dramatic and quick transformation of the German people and their country. To-day, they are united as one people and have built one of the most prosperous economies in Europe.

I went to Berlin as the wall was coming down and helped chisel away at the thick concrete. I brought back a large piece in my suitcase. I keep it as a reminder to not let resentments take root in my mind and create barriers that limit my good.

If you want to access the power of your mind and create the life of your dreams, you will have to get rid of the twelve-foot-high, electrified barbed-wire fence. Your mind was never intended to hold resentments, just as your body was not designed for disease. Both of them are unnatural and prevent you from living well and happily.

I Haven't Got Time for the Pain

Carly Simon wrote a hit that I used to claim as my theme song. It was titled "Haven't Got Time for the Pain." When I would get hurt by something mean someone said or cruel thing they did, I would sing that song at the top of my lungs. My intention was to immediately put the pain behind me and move on. Taking no time to feel it, I would just forge ahead.

This strategy worked for a long time until one day I caught myself driving in traffic like a maniac, honking at others, screaming profanities and flipping people off. After one of these road rage events, I suddenly became conscious of my behavior. Knowing it was unusual for me to act in such an abrupt manner, I sat quietly and asked myself, "Why are you so angry?"

It took a while for me to answer truthfully. What came to mind at first were petty rationalizations. My answer was: "I'm angry because people are stupid. They don't drive right." As I dug deeper into the real reason for my anger, the answer came: "Sometimes it's just a lot easier to stay angry than it is to be hurt." I was putting a thin veneer of anger over a thick layer of unprocessed pain. Without my taking time to feel the pain and disappointment that comes from everyday human life, that pain had turned to anger and reared its ugly head to get my attention.

What I learned is that if you don't take time to feel it, you can't ever heal it. If you never take time to process the disappointment and mourn the loss, those feelings remain in your heart and may cause you to act out in inappropriate ways. Avoiding the pain may seem like a good strategy at first, but in the end all it does is prolong the hurt and prevent the healing.

When is the last time you could honestly say, "I am really happy"? Do you remember the last time you felt true joy? Some people have to go all the way back to childhood to recall that day. The reason children laugh more than adults and experience more joy is because they're unencumbered by the weight of resentment and past hurt. They laugh when they're happy and cry when they're hurt. They process their feelings without delay.

I saw an example of this take place recently in an upscale restaurant on a busy holiday weekend. Every table in the restaurant was filled with people dressed up in their finest Easter garments. A couple was seated at a table nearby with their young daughter, who was all decked out in a pretty pink dress. She appeared to be about ten years old and it was obvious that she was very happy wearing her dress. She kept playing with the ruffles and adjusting its fluffy pink fabric.

After the waitress seated the family, she put a paper place mat in front of the little girl and gave her crayons to draw a picture. The child quickly began creating her masterpiece. Every few minutes she would hold it up and present it to her father to gain his approval.

The waitress returned with the drinks and placed them on the table. The girl had apparently ordered a Coke and when she went to pick it up, it slipped through her little hands and 16 ounces of cola spilled all over her artwork and onto her dress.

From the sound that came out of her mouth, you'd have

thought she was in horrible pain. She watched helplessly as her artwork was ruined and her pretty pink dress was drenched and stained. It was quite a scene. The parents jumped up from their seats. The waitress came over and made a hurried attempt to clean up the mess. And the little girl just cried and cried. Nothing could console her. In her mind, it was the end of the world. Her precious art was ruined. Her pink dress was desecrated.

I watched as her father became increasingly uncomfortable because she wouldn't stop crying. Both parents seemed embarrassed as other patrons looked on. The father leaned in and told his little girl to stop crying. But nothing could end her sorrow. She had no concern for social propriety.

In a few minutes, the table was reset. The mess got cleaned up and little girl was given a new place mat and more crayons to start drawing again. In no time, the tears were over and she happily returned to making art. She was giggling and playing again as if nothing had ever happened.

Watching this scene made me wonder how much better the world would be if everyone were as emotionally honest as that little girl. How much healthier would we be if we cried when we're sad and laughed when we're happy?

As inconvenient and even socially inappropriate as it may be, openly and honestly expressing your emotions is always the healthy thing to do. It prevents you from becoming a member of the walking wounded, those people who get up every new day carrying around yesterday's pain and hurt.

Human life can be rough. Our feelings get hurt. People can be cruel. Life is unjust. Getting hurt is unavoidable. Being disappointed is part of our everyday experience. But that doesn't mean we're supposed to collect our hurts and carry them through life. Nor are we supposed to build up resentments, holding on to our anger year after year.

Beneath the anger, and just below the pain, is a deep well of joy. It lies at the center of your being. It is your true and natural state of being. It's what Spirit created you for. To return to joy, you must express your feeling nature and emote your emotions. They were not designed to be controlled or repressed.

If you don't take time to listen to the anger and feel the pain, you'll never get to that deep well of joy within you. Take time for the pain. Express it. Cry. Feel the hurt. Let it break your heart. Be angry. Say what you need to say to whoever hurt you. Be honest.

You have a right to your feelings. Express them in a productive way without lashing out and hurting others. Making others hurt because you are hurting is not the solution. It will only perpetuate the pain and prevent you from moving forward.

You are a powerful being, designed to live freely. Your spirit must be kept light. It cannot move through life easily and joyfully if you insist on carrying around the emotional baggage of the past. The only way to permanently release the past is to forgive.

Forgive But Don't Forget

You probably have good reasons to hold on to your resentments. You might have been a victim of a crime or some great injustice. Perhaps you were raised in a dysfunctional family. Maybe your best friend betrayed you. It is impossible to pass through human life and not get hurt. Everyone has a story to tell of pain and hardship. Some are more dramatic than others.

And it's because we've been hurt that we feel so righteous about our resentments. Somehow we think our feelings of anger and hurt will make those who hurt us pay for what they did. And yet, just the opposite occurs. Such feelings infect our own lives and do nothing to the person who hurt us. I heard someone say that resentment is like taking poison every day and waiting for the other person to die. Our attempt to take vengeance on them ends up hurting only ourselves.

Everything that has happened to you has brought you to

the person you are today. You may have been hurt. You may have been abused. But you survived it. Warts and all, wounds and all, somehow you made it through. And now you are at the most powerful place in your life, the point of choice. Will you let what happened prevent you from moving forward in life? Will you let it take your joy and delay your good? Or will you choose to forgive and move on? What happened is in the past. Now only you can decide your future.

Forgiveness is a gift you give to yourself. It is an act of self-love. It does nothing to the person who hurt you. It's a decision you make *about* yourself *for* yourself. Choosing to forgive doesn't mean you will forget what happened to you. On the contrary, it allows you to take the wisdom you gained from the hurtful situation and leave the pain and anger behind.

Forgiveness is not about forgetting. It is not about condoning poor behavior or making allowances for abusive people. It doesn't rationalize their behavior or give them approval to hurt you again. Forgiveness isn't about *them*. It's about you.

You may have had good reasons to hold on to your feelings of anger and resentment, but none of them can equal the benefits of letting go. Here are just a few:

SEVEN BENEFITS OF FORGIVING

1. It allows you to put the pain of the past behind you.
2. It releases your spirit to move forward.
3. It invites new opportunities.
4. It attracts love.
5. It removes the obstacles to your growth.
6. It attracts wealth.
7. It is empowering.

Take Your Power Back

I went to the family reunion of my partner this past summer. There were nearly a hundred people in attendance on a hot day in August in a small Texas town. The patriarch of the family is my partner's father, a proud eighty-six-year-old man married for fifty-nine years to his wife, who recently passed away. Both of them worked hard to provide for their large family of eight children.

Even though I have visited my partner's family only a few times in the nearly twenty years we've been together, what most impressed me about his parents is how they love all of their children unconditionally. They may not understand all of their choices, nor approve of them, but that never stopped them from loving them. Very few people have the spiritual maturity to know that understanding is not a pre-requisite for loving.

The day before the reunion was to take place, one of my partner's relatives sent an e-mail to the entire family saying he would not be in attendance. His reason for not coming was that I would be there. In his correspondence, he said that he had been in conversation with God and had concerns for his mortal soul. Because he didn't approve of what he referred to as my "lifestyle," he decided it would be best to not come to the family reunion.

Even though I have spoken to this man only once or twice in my life, he felt so threatened by my presence that he denied himself the opportunity to be with the rest of the family. My first thought was, "Wow! He's given me a lot of power. He's given me complete control over his thoughts and actions."

Fortunately, his choice didn't prevent me, or my partner, from enjoying the reunion. In fact, no one in attendance seemed to be adversely affected by his absence. It was unfortunate that he denied himself such a golden opportunity to be with his family. I pray it will not be the last chance he had to see my partner's father alive.

Resentment is powerful. It gives all of your power over to the person you condemn. They have taken over your mind. They are in control of your feelings. They dictate your actions. Without knowing it, you have become their victim.

Forgiveness means taking your power back. It is a bold and courageous act to not let those who've hurt you steal your joy and invade your peace of mind. It draws a line in the sand by saying, "I am not willing to spend another day of my life hurt or angry. You may have hurt me once, but I'll be damned if I let you do it again!"

Forgiveness is a personal declaration of independence. It separates your future from the past. It reinstates your own authority. No longer are you willing to relinquish control of your thoughts or feelings to someone else. You regain your ability to create your own future without dragging around past infections, pain and regret. It severs the link, once and for all, between you and those who hurt you.

The Incredible Hulk

Years ago I counseled a young teenage boy named Kevin (not his real name) who was referred to me as a "throwaway child." Apparently that's the label given to unwanted children who've been abandoned by their parents. After years of neglect and being handed down from one home to the next, Kevin had grown angry and was acting out at school.

At our first meeting, he seemed unusually calm and mild-mannered. So, I asked him, "What makes you angry?" And he replied, "I don't usually get angry." I continued my inquiry and asked, "Well, how is it that you're getting into so much trouble in school? What's the cause of that?" His answer was quite interesting. He said, "I have this button that goes off. It's kind of like a switch that kicks in, similar to the Incredible Hulk. Everything's going along fine and then something pisses me off, the button gets pushed and I go into a rage!" I said, "That's funny. I don't have a button like that. Where did you get it?"

When children don't feel loved, they get angry. They act out. If this pattern isn't recognized and healed early on, it gets carried into adulthood and can become a catalyst for violent behavior and criminal activity. That's why there are so many young men in prison. They began as throwaway children, abandoned by their parents or society.

After a few more appointments and when he felt he could trust me, Kevin finally admitted that the focus of his anger was his mother. He was furious that she had abandoned him. She was the cause of the button that turned him into the Incredible Hulk. He said he just couldn't understand how a mother could treat her only son in such a lousy way. I knew that if he didn't process his anger, he'd never get to the pain and sadness beneath it and find his way to healing, so I encouraged him to write her a letter and bring it to our next session. He began the letter with the words "Dear bitch."

After Kevin wrote several more enraged letters, he finally got to the sadness beneath his anger. I watched and consoled him as he cried for not having been loved. We talked about the injustice of his situation. "It's not fair," he said. And I agreed. "It's not fair. Your mother *should* have loved you. She should have taken care of you. It's not right. Now you have a choice," I told him. "You can spend your adult life angry about not being loved by your mother and have that anger get you into a lot of trouble. Or, you can get the love she didn't give you somewhere else. Either way, your future as an adult will be created from that choice."

Kevin understood. We talked a lot about choices. He mourned his loss and moved on. And the switch that turned him into the Incredible Hulk eventually got turned off.

Kevin fell victim to a common error that a lot of people make. When their needs aren't met in one place, instead of looking for them to be met in another, they get stuck in the anger and injustice of their situation. That's kind of like knocking on one door, having someone open it, slap you and slam the door in your face. And instead of going to another door where someone may embrace you, you knock on the same door again. Of course, the abuser opens the door, slaps you again and slams the door in your face. This happens time and time again, with you standing outside the door, continuing to knock, getting more and more frustrated and angry. The solution, of course, is to stop knocking on that door. You are in a hallway with a thousand other doors. Behind all the other doors are people waiting to love and embrace you. Try a new door!

The Process of Forgiveness

I think more people might be willing to forgive if they knew how to get started. There is much written about the importance of forgiveness, but little about how to do it. Even when we understand the benefits of forgiveness and are ready to tackle it, most people just don't know where to begin.

As convenient as it may be, unfortunately there aren't easy steps to follow that will get you to the moment when you can say, "I'm done. I have forgiven them. I am free." Forgiveness is more of a process. It's a journey to undertake, not a destination that you can rush to. This is especially true when the person you are attempting to forgive is yourself.

Generally speaking, the first issue that needs to be addressed in our effort to forgive is communication. As I told one woman who was physically abused by her parents, "If your parents had seen who you *really* are, if they could have seen the pure presence of God within you, they would have never laid a hand on you."

If Kevin's mother had seen or known the value of her own

life, she would have never abandoned her son and turned him into the Incredible Hulk. Our inability to see each other or communicate ourselves fully is what leads to a breakdown in relationships, causing anger and resentment. Resentment issues usually begin with a breakdown in communication.

Use the exercise below to begin the healing process of forgiveness.

EXERCISE: FORGIVENESS WRITING

Thoughts of anger and feelings of resentment block the flow of good into your life. Your mind must be kept free and clear for you to live happily and successfully. Your feelings must be expressed openly and honestly in order for you to be the powerful being Nature designed you to be.

Sit in the silence for a few minutes. Ask the question: Am I harboring resentment for someone? If so, whom? Am I angry? If so, what is the source of my anger? After taking time for inner reflection, write a letter to that person or express your feelings in a journal. Repeat this process until you feel you have expressed everything in your heart.

As with Kevin, sometimes your first communication will be about venting anger. I think we all probably need to write more letters that begin with the words "Dear bitch"! Whether you actually mail or e-mail the letter is an entirely different issue. Remember: This isn't about them. It's about *you*. It's *your* thoughts and feelings that must be released to free you from the past.

Once you've written one letter, write another. And continue writing until you get to the sadness and feelings of loss just beneath the anger. Those feelings are in your heart. You may have plastered over them with anger and held them down for years, but they will surface if you allow space. When they rise to the surface, give yourself time to process them. You have to feel it to heal it.

What Is Your True Commitment?

Taking the journey to forgiveness requires commitment. The process of clearing your mind of anger and hurt takes time. It doesn't generally happen overnight. This is particularly true if you've been holding on to resentment for many years. It's our self-righteousness that usually gets in the way. We know the question we have to answer is: "Do you want to be right, or do you want to be happy?" We just want both, so our little ego-self answers: "Yes, I want to be right *and* I want to be happy."

But we can't have both. We have to be committed to one or the other. To me, the right choice seems clear. I'd much rather be happy than right. Happiness just seems to last longer.

What are you committed to? What kind of life do you want to live? Do you want to be happy? Do you want to be successful in love and career? Do you want to be healthy and prosperous? If so, you will have to commit yourself to the daily maintenance of your mind. Like a summer vegetable garden that requires daily weeding, you must sort through the negative thoughts and resentful feelings and remove them from your mind. Just like the garden, if you don't maintain your mind by tending to it daily, the weeds will outgrow it in no time at all.

Forgiveness is hard work. It requires diligence and commitment. It forces you to grow up and accept responsibility for your own experience in life. It fuels spiritual growth. The end product is a healthy and happy life, but the process in getting there is not for the weak-minded. The key is to be more committed to your own happiness than in holding on to the "You should have" and "You owe me."

Nobody Knows the Trouble I've Seen

I think people eventually tire of being angry. At some point, hearing yourself blame others for your limitations will become rote and boring. When you've told your woeful tale so many times that you've begun to elaborate on the details and enhance them for dramatic effect, you know you're more committed to repeating the drama than you are to healing it. I happen to know that from my own personal experience.

In my early twenties, as a full-grown man but still a psychological and spiritual infant, I thought the most interesting thing about my life was all of the agony I survived as a child. Meeting someone new who hadn't heard my miserable tale was like giving fresh meat to a tiger. I couldn't wait to corner them across a dinner table or at a club so I could tell them all of my excuses for not living up to my potential. "It's my mother's fault," I'd say. "She wasn't a responsible adult and lacked parenting skills." Then I'd share all of the details of being raised by a woman who had very little maternal instinct. "It's my father's fault," I'd say. "He was emotionally absent and never really connected with his children." He was my excuse for failed relationships. "I had no functional role models," I would tell them. On and on I went, outlining the gory details of the story, pausing only for dramatic effect when necessary.

After doing this for many years, I noticed that my story was losing effect. The people I shared it with seemed less and less interested in hearing it. In fact, some would interrupt me with tales of their own misery, at which point I would quickly work to convince them my own sadness and suffering was much greater than theirs. It became a dueling game of who suffered the most. Unconscious of the effect this was having on my life, I continued to regurgitate the same old story until one day someone I had known for many years rudely said to me, "God! I'm so tired of hearing you tell that story! Why don't you get a new one?" I was deeply offended.

Somebody said the truth will set you free, but first it will piss you off. Well, I was definitely pissed off at the truth bearer who had the audacity to tell me to get a new story. And yet something in me knew he was right. I had been telling that story for way too long. Even I was getting bored with it.

Further education and spiritual practice eventually helped

me lose interest in telling that old story from my past. I stopped gaining value from being a victim. I didn't want to be the winner in the game of who's suffered the most. Plus, I found that people are much more interested in hearing about your dreams than your drama. So I started talking about my vision for the world and the dreams I wanted to see manifest.

Lurking in the crevices of most people's mind is the twisted notion that somehow our lives are made better by suffering. We wear our wounds like Boy Scouts wear their badges, proudly featuring them for others to see. We take too much pride in surviving the worst and not enough in making the best.

Maybe it's part of the culture. Perhaps we get the idea from religion. Whatever the case, there is no truth to the belief that people are improved by surviving misery. Suffering is not imposed by God. It doesn't build character. Suffering doesn't purify your soul or make you stronger or wiser. All it does is diminish your spirit.

SEVEN QUESTIONS TO ASK YOURSELF

1. Am I more interested in being right than I am in being happy?
2. Am I ready to face my feelings and feel the anger and pain of being hurt?

3. Am I fully committed to releasing my resentment toward the person or situation that hurt me?
4. Am I willing to stop telling my story about what hurt me?
5. Am I willing to stop putting the other person down and assassinating his or her character?
6. Am I willing to let go of anything necessary to live a happy, healthy life?
7. Am I willing to stop blaming others and making excuses for not living up to my potential?

You never really grow up until you take full responsibility for the quality of your own life. As long as you are blaming your parents, the government, ex-wife or husband, you're still an infant who never fully matured. Stop telling your story. Grow up. Get over it. Move on. Be more committed to building a future than you are to surviving a past. That's the key to accessing the power of you.

Owner's Manual

I wish you'd been given an owner's manual when you were born. If you had, it would have been titled *Your Mind and How to Use It—An Owner's Manual*. The manual would have the following content:

LESSON ONE: You don't really have a mind; you use a Mind.

LESSON TWO: There is no Off switch, so stop looking.

LESSON THREE: You will hear voices. You're not going crazy.

LESSON FOUR: Think about things that bring you joy.

LESSON FIVE: Stay tuned. More will come.

LESSON SIX: The game of life is rigged: Everything works in your favor.

LESSON ONE: You Don't Really Have a Mind; You Use a Mind.

In 1841, Ralph Waldo Emerson published an essay titled "History" in which he wrote: "There is one mind common to all individual men. Every man is an inlet to the same and to all of the same. . . . What Plato has thought, he may think; what a saint has felt, he may feel; what at any time has befallen any man, he can understand."

The thing you call *your* mind is really your connection to the one Mind, the Mind of God: the Creator of the universe.

You are an individual thinker using the one Mind, causing and creating your own individual experience. Your greatest thoughts and works do not come from yourself. They come from accessing the one universal Mind.

Genius doesn't come from men or women. It flows *through* them. Love doesn't come from other people in your life; it comes *through* them. There is only one true source of genius and perfect love. That source is Spirit.

The world's greatest thinkers were accessing the one Mind, processing its genius through their minds. The world's greatest lovers were accessing the love of God emanating from within their hearts. Every new invention or masterpiece of art comes from the same source, the one Mind. Every act of great love or forgiveness comes from the same source, the one unconditional Lover.

Here's how it works: Think of a mainframe computer that each individual computer connects to through the Internet. In your own personal computer, you can create a masterpiece of art, write a romance novel or play games. But your programming comes from the mainframe and your connection through the Internet. It is the source of your power and your connection to knowledge.

This mainframe computer is really the Mind of God. It is the Creator and sustainer of all life throughout the universe.

Within that Mind is the formula for creation itself, the mathematical equation necessary to initiate the Big Bang. Also contained within it is the wisdom of the ages, giving you instant access to all that can be known.

Every day, the Mind of God delivers to *your* mind thoughts that can lead to your greater good. You call them *your* dreams. They are your innate Divine potential. They have been specifically chosen to match your unique character and talent. If you follow them, they will lead you to a life of fulfillment and peace. If you don't follow them, they will haunt you.

LESSON TWO: There Is No Off Switch, So Stop Looking.

You can't turn your mind off. It's your connection to your Creator and cannot be severed. Unlike some unreliable Internet connections, your mind can never lose contact with the one Mind. That's why you can't stop thinking. Even at night in your dreams, your mind is working. It is creating vivid images and characters. Stories unfold and dramatic scenes play out in an effort to communicate something significant to your conscious self.

Valuable information is being passed back and forth

through your connection to the one Mind. It is a two-way information highway. Consciously or unconsciously, you use this Mind each day. Every thought you have gathers to form your belief system, which causes your experience.

Your dreams, fears, hopes and wishes flow in one direction on one side of the information highway. They are received by the Mind of God as your tendency of thought and are acted upon immediately. Resources are gathered, circumstances created, people come forward to manifest that which you have believed in.

Coming back to you from the other direction on the two-way road is wisdom, direction, advice and the answer to every question you have. But you must take time to listen so you can hear. By quieting your mind, you will hear the voice of Spirit.

You are having a conversation with God that never ends. From this conversation, your life experience is created.

LESSON THREE: You Will Hear Voices.
You're Not Going Crazy.

You're not going crazy. The voices in your mind are real. Learn to listen to *one* of them and tune out the rest. One of the voices you hear is your Creator. It set up this communication system so you'd never be alone or far away from everything you need to know.

All of the other voices are from the past. They're the fearful monkey chatter of those who've gone before you and lost their way. Sometimes you will hear that voice as your father warning you not to quit a job before you have another. Sometimes it will take the shape of your mother scolding you for being too trusting of others. The voice of fear and doubt can sometimes be heard as your own, casting judgment of others and predicting the worst possible outcome for every situation.

These voices in your mind are the echoes of the billions of people who've lived and died on our world. Their fears and doubts can easily be heard in our own minds and take the form of the inner critic. You can recognize that voice easily by the ugly things it says.

Just as easy to recognize is the voice of your Creator. Though it may have been quieted by your fears and somewhat silenced by the inner critic, it is still active within you. That voice says things like: "You have power within you awaiting your discovery. You can accomplish anything you set your mind to do. Trust me. Follow the dreams I've given you. I will always love you."

If you will listen to that voice, it will lead you to the life of your dreams. Listen closely. Do what it tells you to do. Follow its direction.

LESSON FOUR: Think About Things
That Bring You Joy.

Just as your car was not designed to run on water, your mind was not designed for negative thinking. That's why those thoughts leave you feeling so miserable. If negative thinking were the natural and correct way to use your mind, its effect would be happiness.

If you fill your gas tank with water, you won't get very far. That same truth applies to the use of your mind. If you fill it with thoughts of fear, anger and resentment, you won't get very far in life. You'll stay stuck in neutral, never really moving forward.

You may change jobs to avoid an abusive boss, but you'll attract another one in your new place of employment. You might divorce your spouse because of a failed marriage, but you'll repeat the same mistakes in the next relationship. The more things change, the more they will stay the same. Your inner thinking will always manifest and create your outer experience. So until you change your thinking, you can't really change your life.

Try this: Use your mind the way it was designed to be

used. Think on things that bring you joy. Think about the people you love and why you love them. Think about your best ideas and how they can become manifest. Think about the silly people in your life, the ones that make you laugh out loud.

When you start using your mind the way it's *supposed* to be used, you'll begin to hear your conversations change as well. Instead of the negativity that used to unconsciously spew from your mouth, you'll catch yourself saying positive and encouraging things to others. Instead of expecting the worst, you'll have raised your standards.

From thoughts follow actions. From actions follow experience. Your life is literally created one thought at a time. You have access to the force that can change everything. It is your mind, and every thought you choose creates an experience that exactly mirrors it. So choose wisely.

If you want to find your way back to your Creator through the maze of human drama and confusion, follow joy. Your heart is connected to your mind. By following what makes your heart sing, you'll find God.

LESSON FIVE: Stay Tuned. More Will Come.

Your mind and the Mind of God are inextricably linked. Your Creator is always sending information to you through the link it established. If you take time to listen, it will guide you every step of the way. It will answer every question in your mind. It will tell you everything you need to know to find love and create success.

We spend too much time talking to God and not enough time listening. Because most people think of themselves as the highlight of God's concern, they update the Creator on all of their affairs in their nightly prayers. They say things like, "Well, God, today I had a tough time at work. And did I tell you I was thinking about moving to another apartment?" Sometimes this nightly update becomes a game of *Let's Make a Deal*. We promise we'll treat our family members better or give more money to charity if God will do something for us in return.

The spiritually immature tend to be self-absorbed. They think only of their own needs. So it's no wonder they would look to the heavens thinking their desires are the most important thing on God's Mind. Our concept of God is so primitive that we actually think the Infinite Mind that sustains life in the universe has a preference as to whether we live in one particular apartment or choose one job over another, when nothing could be further from the truth.

God's desire for your life is the same as it is for everyone it creates. And that is for you to be happy, experience love and be all that you want to be. The particulars you choose yourself. The Creator didn't make one person who has the capacity to love you, cut you in half and randomly toss your "other half" somewhere on earth for you to hunt down. What kind of diabolical plan would that be? There are millions of people who have the capacity to love you. Not just one. God didn't give you just one talent to be used in a career. You are a multifaceted creative individual. There are lots of things you can do to make a living and fulfill yourself.

From a cosmic perspective it doesn't matter where you live, what career you choose or whom you love. All those choices are left up to you. That doesn't mean, however, that God has no interest in your life. Quite the contrary. It is intimately and personally invested in your success. So much so that it will tell you everything you need to know, *if* you will listen.

Our right relationship with Spirit has been outlined in Bible verses. They hint at how we are to connect to the Source of all good things: *Seek and you shall find. Knock and the door will be opened. Ask and it shall be given.* Each one of these verses implies that you must take the first action. You have to do the seeking, knocking and asking.

The first gift of love is freedom. So, God, being *perfect* Love, has set you free in life to make your own choices and pursue your own course. As you journey through life, you may come to a fork in the road and have to make a decision as to which path to take. The path that leads to your best life is known in the Mind of God. If you will take time to ask, you will receive an answer. However, you can choose not to access that Mind and go it alone.

Everything you need to do to attract love, build wealth and be healthy is known in the Mind of God. It is behind the door. But you have to *knock* on that door. You have to seek in order to find. As odd as it may seem, God's policy is: Don't ask, don't tell.

LESSON SIX: The Game of Life Is Rigged: Everything Works in Your Favor.

You are not alone. You never will be. Within your heart and mind is the Spirit that created you. It dwells within and yet also surrounds and embraces you. You can never escape its presence. And though it appears that you are separate and alone, appearances are deceiving. There is more to life than can be realized with your limited human senses.

You were created by a perfect Spirit, whose intelligence and power has no end. You are a perfect idea imagined and created by the Mind of God. You have been set free in life to discover the truth of who you are, and yet never for one second have you been left alone. Your journey has brought you this far. Now you are conscious. Now you are awake. Now you have your power back.

Because there is only one Spirit, consciously creative and perfect in every way, success is guaranteed. In many ways the game of life is rigged in your favor. You may struggle for a while. You may have your little failures, but in the end you will have what your heart longs for. You will find the love you seek. You will be your true authentic self. You will claim your glory.

The Creator is in love with you, its beloved creation, so learn to trust. Everything works in your favor.

What Were You Thinking?

In 1995, it was widely reported that English actor Hugh Grant was arrested in Los Angeles for lewd conduct in a public place with an alleged Hollywood prostitute. It was unfortunate timing. The arrest occurred just two weeks before the release of his first major studio film, *Nine Months*, which he was in town promoting.

The *Tonight Show with Jay Leno* had him booked for an appearance that same week, and despite his embarrassing situation, Hugh kept his appointment. When Mr. Leno introduced him to the audience and he was seated, Jay turned to him and asked, "What were you thinking?" The obvious answer is: He *wasn't* thinking.

You are the thinker choosing your thoughts. You have total control over the one and only thing you can change in life: your own mind and how you use it. You can think any way you please. You can believe anything you like. You can take any action. But you must accept the results of those choices.

The fact is, we don't always make good choices. We are not bad people. We are good people who sometimes make bad choices. But even then, the tuition we pay is worth the high cost as long as we learn something of value. Some choices are clear. They announce themselves through our intuition. Others aren't so clear, so we muddle our way through by trial and error. In either case, we learn something we can use on the road ahead.

If you haven't always made good choices, don't waste time beating yourself up. The world hasn't come to an end. You're still alive. Plus, you gained something from every choice you've made, even if it was just the wisdom to never make that choice again. Hugh Grant and many others who've made bad choices have gone on to experience great success. You can too. The sooner you let go of the past, the faster you will move forward.

With practice, you will learn to choose thoughts that create the results you want in life. In time, you will begin making choices with greater wisdom. Be patient with yourself as you grow.

Great Minds

Eleanor Roosevelt has been quoted as saying, "Great minds discuss ideas; average minds discuss activities; small minds discuss people." We tend to discuss whatever it is we're thinking about. So you can use her scale to see what kind of person you are by determining what thoughts you usually entertain.

If you're great, you're thinking about ideas. You are receptive to the infinite Mind of God and fascinated by its endless creativity. Your mind is an open channel to the Divine. Every day a new idea is delivered. And you spend most of your time thinking and talking about your best ideas, greatest new creations and future dreams. Great people aren't born into the world. They're not biological anomalies. Greatness comes from how you use your mind, from what you give your heart to.

According to Eleanor's scale of greatness, if you're just average, you spend a lot of time thinking about activities.

That's what most people think and talk about. The average Joe on the street is using the infinite creative power of his mind to think about where he's going to go after work, what he might do on vacation or order to eat in a restaurant.

And then finally, we can't forget the small-minded, be-cause there are so many of them out there in the world. Small-minded people think and talk incessantly about other people. And if you don't think the media knows that, think again. That's why there are so many readers of tabloid mag-azines and why reality TV is so popular. That's why celebri-ties have millions of Twitter followers. Small-minded people are obsessed with talking about other people.

Most people use their minds like a bunch of monkeys set free in the control room of a nuclear power plant, jumping around pushing buttons, completely unaware of the im-mense power they are using. But you're not one of them. You're not unconscious anymore. You can't pretend that what you think and how you act doesn't matter. You know you have power. You just have to learn to direct it.

Be Like Jack

You have at your disposal a creative Power that knows no limit and now it's time to direct it. The key to creating what you want in life is to learn how to focus your thought. Use your mind like a camera lens. Focus in on what you want to see become manifest. Turn the lens until the image is crystal clear. Now take a mental picture of it and hold it in your mind.

My dog, Jack, is a great teacher for focusing attention. When he hears the jar open that has his puppy treats in it, he comes running into the kitchen. When he sees me take one out of the jar, his eyes become fixed on it. He won't move. He's hyper-focused on what he wants and cannot be distracted.

If I move the hand that holds the treat to the right, his eyes will follow it. If I move my hand to the left, he does the same. Nothing else is in his world but that bacon-flavored piece of heaven. And he will not take his attention off it until he's got it in his mouth.

Be like Jack. Keep your attention focused on what you want. Never take your eyes off of it. Don't be distracted by the fearful voices of others. They have lost faith and want you to do the same. Don't listen to them. Keep thinking about what you want. As you wake up each day, remind yourself that the full creative Power of the universe is at work to manifest your desire.

Think about what you want and want what you think about. Give all your attention to your best ideas. Listen to that one voice within you, the one that says: "I love you. You can do this. I believe in you." It will take time, but your efforts will pay off in the end. You will get to watch your dreams come true.

The negative voices are going to be with you every moment of your life, spinning around in your head. They come with the planet. They're part of the ozone layer of race consciousness. When you stop listening to them, they grow more and more faint, and the voice of Spirit gets louder and louder. That's how you'll know you're on the right track—when instead of saying, "You're not good enough. You can't make it," the voice inside you says, "Behold my Power to make all things new!"

EXERCISE:
USING YOUR MIND TO
CREATE WHAT YOU WANT

Focus your attention on something you would like to have in your life. Get a clear idea of what it looks like. Involve your senses. What does it feel like to have it? What does it smell like?

If you have artistic skills, draw a picture of it. If not, cut out pictures in magazines and glue them to a piece of cardboard or paper to create a vision board. You may even choose to download images from the Web and create a digital version. Keep the vision in front of you every day for ninety days. Look at it daily and remind yourself that the Power that creates universes is at work manifesting your dreams.

Use the prayer below. Say it aloud each day after looking at your vision board.

I live, move and have my being in a Presence and Power that knows no limit. That Presence is the indwelling Spirit of God. Its desire is for me to experience love, be healthy, vital and successful. My best ideas are delivered to me from the perfect Mind of God. I use the power of my mind to focus my attention faithfully on the ideas I want to see manifest.

Like a seed planted in soil, which automatically begins to grow, my best ideas are planted in Mind and immediately begin to take shape and form. I believe. I have faith. I release. Amen.

Now What?

Like Dorothy in *The Wizard of Oz* who went through great trials and tribulations only to discover the power to take her home was always within her reach, you are realizing your power. You're becoming aware that life isn't just a random event. It is a co-created experience between you and Spirit. You are awakening to the power of you, the power you've always had to create your life.

Nothing is more exciting than to realize you are in control of your own fate. You make your own choices. You use the power of your mind to create your own experience. It's very empowering to know you never have to be a victim again. And yet, instead of creating greater clarity, sometimes this awakening can cause confusion. Now that you're awake and conscious of your power, what's next? What do you do?

It's important to get your own affairs in order first. Heal your relationships. Forgive others who've hurt you. Clear your mind of resentments. Accept and love yourself as you are. Use your God-given talent to create a more prosperous life.

There will always be more spiritual work to be done in your own house. None of us is ever *done*. There will always be some new hurt to heal or challenge to over-come. The question remains, however: Is there some *greater* purpose to your life? Is there some reason you're alive at this time in history? Does your soul have an assignment?

five

Your Soul's Assignment

I hear a lot of people in their forties and fifties say, "I still don't know what I want to be when I grow up." And I always want to say to them: "Well, the first thing to do is to actually grow up!" The first step on the spiritual journey is to mature out of victim-consciousness. It is to assume full responsibility for your experience in life and stop blaming others. Growing up means taking the helm and using your power.

The second step is to realize that the way you use your power matters to others. It contributes to the quality of life on the planet. The thoughts you think don't just affect *your* life. They affect us all. Your actions provide an example to others. Like a stone dropped in a still pond, they send ripples out affecting everyone in their path. The way you live your life matters. It leaves an impression on the planet and affects every soul born after you.

Sometimes that's hard for people to accept because it brings with it so much responsibility. That's why there are always more walking wounded in the world than the consciously creative. We'd like to pretend that what we think doesn't matter and the choices we make don't affect others.

But you can only pretend for a short while. You can't keep your head in the sand forever. Eventually you're going to have to be what God created you to be, and stop pretending you're little and powerless. Eventually you'll have to set your fear aside and face your destiny.

And quite frankly, that scares the hell out of us. We're afraid of our power and potential. We're not afraid of failure. We're afraid of success. We're not afraid to live an *ordinary* life. We fear the *extraordinary* life, the life of greatness.

Ralph Waldo Emerson wrote, "God will not have his work made manifest by cowards." Eventually, to fully express your unique way of being and to find your soul's purpose, you will have to overcome this fear and accept the position your Creator has made for you.

Deep within is your soul's assignment. It was inscribed on your heart when you were created. It is the dream you have always dreamt. It is the vision you have secretly held within you. It is the thing you are called to do, but may slightly fear doing. It is Spirit, alive in your soul, knowing what's possible for your life.

Like the flower that naturally turns to the sun for its source of nourishment, one day you will choose to turn inward, where Spirit resides, and it's there where you will discover your soul's assignment. That's where you'll sense what Spirit created you to be. You won't find your destiny *outside* of you. You won't read it in a book or hear it on television. God is a spiritual Presence that lives inside your soul. It has an internal guidance system that will lead you to your calling, if you will listen.

There's something you're supposed to be doing here. There's a purpose to your life. And it's not necessarily a career or a job. It's a *calling*. It's what your heart knows is yours to do. And here's a clue: It may be what you keep wishing someone else would do.

Our soul assignments don't always arise from our dreams or fantasies. Sometimes they come from things that upset or disturb us, things we wish were different in the world, as was the case with Dr. Martin Luther King Jr. and Burmese political prisoner Aung San Suu Kyi, both recipients of the Nobel Peace Prize. Their soul's assignment was activated by an injustice in the world. They were both called to take a stand for what is right.

Pursuing what Spirit calls you to do may or may not make

you popular. That's why it's important to not mistake your soul's assignment for an ego agenda. It has nothing to do with becoming rich or famous. Fame or fortune may follow, but it must never be your goal.

What Spirit calls you to do isn't necessarily some huge undertaking, like fighting political or social injustice like Aung San Suu Kyi and Dr. King. It may be something rather simple, like letting go of all that blocks love from entering your life, or being an example to others of a person who is conscious and kind.

Never underestimate the value of one person who has learned to live well. One person who knows how to love and can accept love in return can change the world. One parent who can love their children unconditionally affects many generations to come. One person who buoyed themselves above the depths of low self-esteem to full acceptance and self-love provides a positive example to many.

If you can be that one person who lives without conflict in your mind and finds love in your heart, you are of enormous value to the world. Like a single drop of clear, fresh water dropped in a muddy glass, you are making a difference. At first glance, your contribution may not be noticeable, but over time the mud will sink to the bottom and the water will be clear enough to drink.

Spirit has invested heavily in you. The life you call your own isn't really yours. It's the life of God, individualized in your unique character and personality. The body you call yours, the face that reflects in the mirror, isn't really a separate you. It is the face and form of your Creator. The Spirit that animates your body, thinks through your mind and feels through your heart is the one Spirit manifesting all of creation.

We "live and move and have our being" in a field of infinite possibility, in the Presence of a Spirit that knows no end. You are immersed in this field that responds to you by creating an experience that exactly matches the tendency of your thought. Anything is possible.

So as you consider what your Creator has assigned your soul to do in the world, don't be limited by your past. Ignore your current limitations. They have nothing to do with your future. Historically speaking, those who have been called to greatness have had to overcome many obstacles and limitations. Perhaps it is the calling itself that provides the wisdom and courage you need to overcome what appears to limit you.

Your soul's assignment is never to suffer misery or take abuse. Spirit has no need of martyrs. There is no cosmic call to sacrifice your health and well-being for others, nor is there any value gained in doing so. Be sure you're not play-ing the "victim game" that one of my long-suffering friends jokes about when he says, "You take the only lightbulb in the house. I'll just sit here in the dark alone."

You have something no one else has in the world. You see things differently. Your thoughts are original. Your heart loves like no other. Your Creator threw away the mold after you were born. Your soul's destiny is tied to that unique-ness. When looking for my own, a wise friend asked me, "What's the one thing people have said about you your en-tire life?" All I could think of is what my parents and teach-ers said throughout my childhood. Every one of them said, "Chris, that mouth of yours is going to get you into trouble one of these days!"

I am a speaker. I make my living teaching and coaching others. Instead of getting me into trouble, my mouth be-came the tool I use to verbalize thought. What the adults around me saw as a defect in my personality was really just an untrained and undiscovered asset.

Ultimately, nothing will bring you peace but expressing fully who you are. Until that day, you are living only half a life. You're a shell of a body walking around with an enor-mous amount of unrealized potential, untapped and unused. Isn't it time you started to explore the depths of your being? Aren't you getting tired of living small and accepting less?

You have been set free on a journey of discovery. Now that you have awakened to your power, it's time to take the next step. It's time to find and fulfill your soul's assignment.

How Do You Define Success?

To find what your true purpose is in life requires some inner reflection and thought. To begin, it's important to answer the questions: How do I define success? What makes me feel accomplished and satisfied at the end of the day?

I used to work for a furniture store that specialized in Italian imports. The high-styled furniture was shipped in via container from Europe. The American buyers would make semi-annual trips to Italy to make the purchases they felt would best sell to our customers. One time, the opposite occurred. The Italians came to America. This was their first trip to our country, so I was anxious to get their impression. After they had been in the store two weeks and observed how Americans do business, I asked one of them what he thought. He said, "You Americans work too much! In Italy, we work to have a good life. But here, you have made work your whole life. You talk business all of the time. When do you have time for family and friends? Where is the joy in your life?"

I recall the American buyers' frustration when trying to order from Italian factories in the summer. They were told, "We close the factory in August. It is too hot here. We go to the beach." I remember thinking to myself what a luxury it must be to take an entire month just to spend at the beach.

Perhaps the Italians are right. Maybe we Americans do work too much. Maybe we are so driven by our consumer culture that we believe owning more stuff will make us happy and fulfilled. So our definition of success is to have a bigger house, more luxurious car and all of the latest technology. But what price are we paying for this picture of success? For many, it means living beyond their means, with high credit card debt. For some, it means sacrificing time with their friends and family to spend more time at work.

Many people live unconscious lives, with their eyes fixed on the pavement, forging ahead with no thought of their own. They're just following the person in front of them and doing what they're told. They never stop to think about what *they* want, or what their own picture of success might look like. They go to bed at night tired from working too much and sleeping too little, and get up the next day and do it all over again. Year after year, the pace continues until something happens to wake them from their sleep. Suddenly, they wonder, "Why am I doing this?"

We forget that we are in charge of our own lives, that

we're not just victims. We get to choose how we spend our time and what to give our effort to. Because we are all individuals, we get to define success in our own way. For some, the picture of success is luxury items. They feel successful when they have the benefits of a high income. For others, it involves career and the accolades they receive from the company in which they are employed. Some people feel successful when they have lots of time to spend with loved ones.

You get to create your own picture of success. Don't compare yourself to others when you are defining it in your own mind. We are all in different places at different times in our lives. When I was in my twenties, my definition of success looked very different than it does now that I am in my fifties. When I was younger, success was more work-related. I was climbing the corporate ladder and building a professional résumé. Now, none of that is important to me. Today, my picture of success includes having fun, making a difference in people's lives and having ample time to spend with the people I love.

You have been created as a unique individual. You design your own picture of what a successful life would look like. You get to make it up. Don't let anyone else define it for you. Resist the pull of a society that sells you pictures of what a successful life is supposed to look like on magazine covers and television ads. People never actually feel more successful by having a shinier kitchen floor or because they're able to raise their hands in the air without underarm odor. Those ads may seem ridiculous at first, but in more subtle ways they can affect your self-image.

I had a conversation with a friend recently who was about to turn thirty years old. He said he felt like a failure because he had reached this important milestone in life and hadn't accomplished what he expected. So I asked him, "What did you expect thirty to look like?" And he said, "Well, I certainly expected to be further along in my career by now and at least own a home." My friend has a beautiful wife, loving friends and an active spiritual life. He has worked diligently on healing past addictions and lives a conscious life. He has much to be grateful for and many achievements that can't be measured in mere numbers alone. So I pointed these things out to him and suggested he redefine his picture of success. Maybe it's not about home ownership. Maybe success is a joyful, love-filled life.

Each time there is an economic downturn, our picture of success reveals itself. The news programs will report that some poor soul jumped off a bridge or killed his wife and kids in a violent rage, just because he lost his job and income. It is amazing how challenged people feel when they don't have a regular paycheck coming in. It affects their whole self-concept.

Are we, as the Italians suggested, just income-producing machines? Are we valuable just because we work and make money? Do we have too much of our self-esteem tied to our ability to work?

If you think of yourself as a spiritual being, placed here at this time in history with a unique gift, your picture of success will look very different from those who see themselves just as skilled or unskilled job seekers. You will not define it by increasing numbers on a paycheck. Your picture of success will include work that feeds your soul, not just provides food for your stomach. It will include a perfect outlet for your own unique expression in an environment that inspires you, working with people who respect and honor your gifts. A successful life will include great joy, good health and loving relationships. It will be measured by a sense of accomplishment and a feeling that because you are alive, something got better in the world.

Think clearly about how you must live in order to feel successful. Make sure that you're not being influenced by other people's dreams or expectations for your life. Let go of the need to please others by how you live, or prove to someone else that you are successful. Live by your own standards and definitions. Create your own life and live it consciously.

To get a clearer idea in mind of what a successful life is for you, it's important to start with a vision. A vision is as important to your journey through life as a map is on a road trip. If you don't know where you're going, how can you get there?

The Power of Vision

Why are you alive? What do you have to offer the world? What use are you to God? How are you serving the greater good of all?

You're not here to just sit around taking up space, passing gas. You are supposed to be giving something *to* the world, not just taking from it. You have been born with a purpose. There's a reason your soul has chosen this journey. You must find it.

Successful companies and organizations know the importance of having a vision. It keeps the choices they make in alignment with their purpose and helps communicate their brand to their members or employees. As simple as it may seem, when we know where we're going, it's a lot easier to get there.

When I was in my mid-twenties, I created a personal vision for my life. I wanted to find what my soul's assignment was on earth. I was searching for answers to the great questions: Why did Spirit create me? What purpose does my life serve? Instinctively, I knew there had to be an answer.

Like most of us, we're conditioned to look for answers *outside* ourselves. So I asked around. I talked to successful people. I read a lot of books on the subject of personal vision. I studied philosophy and spirituality. After a great deal of time and research, I didn't find myself one inch closer to my own answer.

That's when I decided to go within. I sat in meditation for thirty days, communing with Spirit, talking and listening. I said, "What is mine to do in the world, God? Lead me to my purpose. Help me realize the potential you placed within me." My practice was thirty minutes a day for thirty days. I was absolutely committed to finding my soul's assignment.

After I had sat several days in meditation, nothing emerged. There was just mindless monkey chatter and a grocery list of things to do. But then about day ten into my thirty-day commitment, ideas started to flood in. So I wrote down the best ideas that came to mind. I had pages and pages of information. When you open your mind to the infinite Mind of God, ideas rush in, unimpeded by fear and doubt.

At the time, I was working in retail management. So when the idea of being a writer came to mind, I didn't give it much credence. Other ideas started to come to light. I had an idea to be a speaker, mentor and coach, even though at the time I had no experience in that area. I decided to let them all surface without judgment. For the next twenty days, an entire world of possibilities and potential gushed out of my head. I was amazed, confused and unclear as to what to do next.

I had a friend who was starting her own business and she gave me some good advice. She said, "Find the common denominator in all of the ideas." So I thought about what all of the ideas coming to my mind had in common. The answer was: They were all about self-expression. Each idea, in its own different way, was about expressing who I am in a manner that would have a positive influence on others.

So that became my personal vision: *Full Self-Expression*. Notice the capital "S" in the sentence. It's my Higher Self that I want to fully express, not the little, ego-self. The vision of Full Self-Expression has been a guiding force in my life for the last thirty years. It makes other choices very clear for me.

For instance, since my vision is Full Self-Expression, I can't be in a relationship with someone who would try to limit my expression or be embarrassed by it. I have to be with someone who will celebrate who I am and respect me. My vision also clarifies what kind of employment I can have. With the vision of Full Self-Expression, I can't work for a company that would put me in a dead-end position or not provide a creative environment. I will thrive if I'm set free to create on my own and not be micromanaged.

Having this vision has made a world of difference in my life. It guides me in every decision I have to make. When faced with a choice, all I have to do is ask: Which choice will allow me to more fully express my Higher Self?

That's the power of vision: It keeps you on course. It becomes a guiding force for all of your decisions about relationship, career and all other choices. It calls on you to let out the potential that's been placed inside by your Creator.

Finding your soul's assignment has to begin with a vision. Until you go within and ask the question "What is my purpose?" you'll just wander around in life, wasting one day after another, ending it without a purpose.

EXERCISE: CREATING A PERSONAL VISION

Sit in meditation for thirty days, taking thirty minutes at each sitting. Ask the following questions:

- What is mine to do in the world?
- What is my purpose?
- What did Spirit create me to do, or be?

- How can I serve the greater good of all humanity?
- What unique gifts do I bring to life?

If answers begin to emerge the first time you use this practice, write them down in a journal or create a document on your computer titled "My Personal Vision." If nothing comes to mind at first, repeat this practice again.

Ideas need time to surface. Sometimes a feeling may emerge instead of a clear idea. If so, describe the feeling as best as you can in your journal or vision document. Don't rush to determine a quick answer. Let your vision emerge in its own time and sequence. There's no rush. Trust the process.

Look for the common denominator in all of the new ideas that are coming to the forefront of your mind. From that commonality, develop your own personal vision statement. Try to narrow it down to as few words as possible, preferably three or four. That makes it easy to remember and clearer to follow.

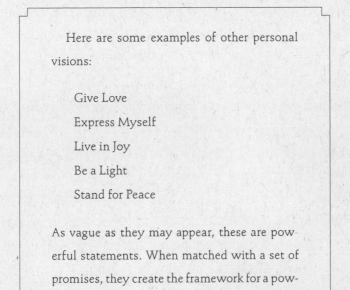

Here are some examples of other personal visions:

> Give Love
> Express Myself
> Live in Joy
> Be a Light
> Stand for Peace

As vague as they may appear, these are powerful statements. When matched with a set of promises, they create the framework for a powerful and dynamic life.

I Promise

When I was a young boy, I expected adults to operate with the utmost integrity. If my parents or a teacher said they were going to do something, I expected them to do it, especially if they said, "I promise." Children can't comprehend paradox and ambiguity. They don't understand that things are rarely black or white.

Generally speaking, there is a fine line of black on one side, a fine line of white on the other, and a huge gray area in between. This is especially true when it comes to human relationships. The choices in life aren't always clear. Nonetheless, even when our lives are full of confusion and uncertainty, we still expect people to do what they say they're going to do. The words *I promise* still mean something to us.

Creating a personal vision is a great step to take to realize your potential and find your soul's assignment. The next step is to create a set of promises that keep you on track. When we make a promise to others, we usually do our best to fulfill it. But sometimes the promises we make to ourselves don't always hold the same weight. That's why New Year's resolutions rarely make it past the first few days of the new year.

The reason they don't work is because we can't act better until we know better. Resolving yourself to a behavior that you haven't prepared for spiritually, emotionally or psychologically will not turn out well. It can put you on a merry-go-round of trying your best, failing and then feeling guilty for failing.

Promises, however, give you an opportunity to set an intention. And if you miss your intention, you can make a new promise. Here are a few examples of the promises I have made myself that follow my personal vision of Full Self-Expression:

1. When I find myself off track and outside the realm of my personal vision, I promise to forgive myself quickly and get back on course.
2. In the midst of confusion or upset, I promise to turn to Spirit first.
3. I promise to participate in some kind of spiritual practice every day.

Notice that promise number one states *when* I find myself off track, not *if*. There's no question that I'm going to wander off. It's my nature to do so. In fact, it's your nature too.

I have a friend who's a pilot for a major airline. He told me that the automatic pilot feature on an aircraft has to make frequent calculations and adjustments just to keep the plane on course to its destination. He said the nature of the aircraft is to go off course.

Like the aircraft, you too have been designed by Nature to go off course. We are not consistent beings. That's why we work out at the gym in the morning and eat ice cream at night. I have a friend who orders the vegetarian burger at a restaurant, but then has the chef add bacon to the top of it for extra flavor. We are ridiculously inconsistent!

Make your first promise to forgive yourself quickly when you go off course. Realize that it is your nature to do so.

Oftentimes the best path to your destination is a zigzag, not a straight line. Going off course allows you to see new things and consider options you hadn't seen before. It's okay to wander off for a while.

EXERCISE: I PROMISE

Once you've created your personal vision, make a set of promises that will help keep you on track. Don't be too ambitious. Keep your promises to just three or four. There's no need for more than that. This isn't about behavior modification. It's about fulfilling your vision.

If you can't think of any promises to make, ask a trusted friend or family member what they think causes you to go off track. They know more about you than they're telling. Give them permission to be honest.

Once you have your personal vision and a set of promises, write them down. Keep them close to you for regular review. They are your brand. They form the basis for who you are and what your life is all about. They lead to your soul's assignment.

Something Is Missing

A woman named Jenna (not her real name) came to me in the late 1990s wanting me to help her find love. She was a corporate executive in her mid-thirties who had spent most of her adult life building a successful career. In her office were all of the accolades, certificates and trophies, proof that she'd done well. But "Something was missing," she told me, "something big."

She said, "I think I'm ready for love. I want an intimate relationship with a man, but not one who's threatened by a woman's success. I want a man who can stand on his own and not be intimidated by me."

Now, it's pretty unusual when someone comes to me that clear on what they want. So I said, "Cool. Let's do some spiritual work to attract into your life the greatest love you've ever known. Let's work together to create a consciousness that will draw the man to you who has the capacity to love and adore you."

I happen to believe love is the easiest thing to attract into our lives. Love is the reason life exists. It's the purpose of the universe. Even though most people are unconscious of it, the truth is, we are embraced and enveloped in the perfect love of Spirit, like a fish swimming in water. Every moment of our lives, we are surrounded by the love and grace of God. So all we have to do to attract love personally is create a true opening for it in our hearts.

Jenna and I went to work immediately. She came to my office once a week for month and we prayed. My prayer was for her to realize the value she had to contribute to an intimate relationship. It was to open her heart to being loved in a personal and special way.

In addition to our spiritual work together, I gave Jenna several take-home assignments. I said, "I want you to make sure you have cleared the way for love to enter your life, and that means be sure you've forgiven any past hurts. Also," I said, "make sure you're not looking to be rescued, because men aren't looking for a damsel in distress these days. They want a true partnership."

Having been to Jenna's house before, I also suggested, "You might want to defeminize your house a bit. Get rid of all those foofy pillows and put away the Hello Kitty merchandise. Take the panty hose off the shower curtain and all the makeup off the counter. Make your house more comfortable for a man. Give him enough room to put a razor and a toothbrush on the bathroom counter."

So she followed my instructions to the letter. She did the spiritual work necessary to forgive her ex-boyfriend of his wrongdoings. She made room in her heart and her house for love. And we kept meeting together week after week doing our prayer work.

But nothing was happening. No results! No man showed up in her life. No one asked her out on a date. Not one single opportunity for love. But she was still committed and confident there would be results, until tragedy struck.

After working together for a month, Jenna called me crying and said, "I have to see you now!" I told her to meet me at my office the next morning. When she walked in, I could see on her face that something was seriously wrong. With her face red and swollen from crying, she poured out the heartbreaking story.

She had been to her doctor for an annual checkup and a lump was discovered in her right breast. After testing, it was determined to be cancerous. The doctor said, "We will have to remove your breast." At the time, sophisticated reconstructive surgery was not an option, so the operation was going to leave her disfigured with one remaining breast.

After telling me her story, she looked me straight in the eyes, with tears running down her face, and asked, "Who's going to love me now? Who's going to love me with one breast?" I said, "Love has an agenda for your life and it won't be stopped by this. Trust me." But I don't think she believed me.

Two weeks later, Jenna had the operation removing her breast. She returned to work and resumed her life and career. She stopped coming to me to pray for love. I guess she just gave up on it. But I never did. I don't give up on love, ever!

Six months passed and I was pleasantly surprised to get a call from her. She told me that she met a man and they had been out on several dates. She said, "I really like this guy." They hadn't been intimate yet because, she said, "I'm just too ashamed of the way I look naked and I'm scared to tell him about the mastectomy."

I said, "Tell him right away. If he's the right guy, it won't matter. And if it matters, he's not the right one." So she took my advice and told him. His response was, "I don't care."

That weekend they took their first trip together. He rented a little cabin up in the mountains for them to stay in. It was fall and all of the leaves were starting to turn colors. There was a little fireplace in the living room, which he lit on their first night. She lay on the floor in his arms, drinking wine and staring at the fire.

And that's when things started to get uncomfortable for Jenna. He went for her blouse. He pulled it down and she pushed it back up. So, he waited a bit and pulled it back down again and she pushed it back up. Men can be rather persistent about these things, so he pulled it down again and she pushed it back up. Finally, he pulled her back in his arms and said, "Why don't you stop trying to hide whatever it is you're trying to hide and just let me love you?"

When she told me this story, tears were coming down her cheeks and she said, "I've never felt a love so complete. I never dreamed anyone could love me that unconditionally." Jenna ended up marrying that man and they just celebrated their fifteen-year anniversary.

The moral of the story is twofold: First of all, when it comes to love, you must *never* give up. Spirit is generous. It has created a variety of people who have the capacity to love you, no matter what condition or shape you are in. Always keep your heart open to love and your mind ready for a new adventure. The Universe has put no limits on your ability to give and receive love, so don't place any on yourself.

Second, as was the case with Jenna, perhaps your soul's assignment is to let yourself be loved fully and completely. Maybe that's why the story of your soul was written. Maybe it's about removing all of the obstacles that have come between you and the life your heart dreams is possible. If so, the vision for your life is simply to Be Love, to experience the depths and heights of it personally.

Every soul has an assignment, a purpose to fulfill. Sometimes that purpose can be found in our dreams. Sometimes it reveals itself in an area of life that is unjust, causing us to take action to make it right. And other times it shows up as a *missing piece*, something our hearts long for that's not there.

EXERCISE: WHAT DO YOU WANT?

Very few people give much thought to what they want in life. They don't think about their desires because they don't really believe they can be fulfilled. Unfortunately, that strategy becomes a self-fulfilling prophecy. Because your mind is the creative element used to create your experience, if you don't use it to think about what you want, it will never show up.

What do you want that you don't have? What is *missing* from your life? What excites

you? What is your dream? Barring any limitations, what do you want to do with your life?

Create a document titled "100 Things I Want
to Do, Be or Have." Challenge yourself to complete the full list of a hundred. Stretch your
imagination. Then choose the top ten. Add
them to your bucket list and commit yourself
to their manifestation.

This exercise will help you get clearer on
your soul's assignment. There have been clues
left inside you. Accessing your desires will lead
you to them.

The Creative Era You Live In

In October 2010, a young twenty-five-year-old guy named
Kevin Systrom launched a new photo-sharing application
called Instagram. It became wildly popular as a newly
emerging social media app. Today it has approximately a
hundred million users, 50 percent of whom are between the
ages of eighteen and thirty-four years old. Actually, it's a ridiculously simple format. All you do is load pictures from
your smartphone and follow others who do the same. Then

you can comment on each other's photos. The genius, however, is in its simplicity.

Apparently, this free app posed such a business threat to Facebook that in April 2012, before the company went public, Facebook founder Mark Zuckerberg bought Instagram for one billion dollars and parked it. The payout to the now twenty-seven-year-old Kevin Systrom was four hundred million dollars. Not bad for a couple of years work, right?

In his groundbreaking book, *The Rise of the Creative Class*, Richard Florida wrote, "Creativity has come to be the most highly prized commodity in our economy." We have left the Information Age behind and entered into a new Creative Era. Kevin Systrom and his new business partner, Mark Zuckerberg, are members of a new type of entrepreneurs called the *creative class*.

You are fortunate enough to live in an amazing time. This new Creative Era brings opportunities to your life that you've never had before. Never before have you been less dependent on corporations and government for your own success. Like Kevin Systrom and Mark Zuckerberg, your greatest good and highest success is now dependent on one thing and one thing alone: your own creative potential, or what I call your connection to the genius Mind of God.

Those who are the most innovative and creative, the ones who understand the power of a new idea, will thrive in this new era. Today's career isn't about gathering information. That may have been true in the latter part of the twentieth century, but not so today. Today's most lucrative career is about delivering value and creative content to the marketplace.

The Creative Era is shrinking the planet, cutting across national borders and creating enormous economic opportunities for people all over the world. Perhaps John Lennon's vision for the world is coming true: Imagine no countries, no borders, no government and no corporations that can restrict or confine your success. Imagine that the only thing you depend on for your livelihood is your own creativity.

The Creative Era is part of the evolution of humanity. As we evolve and mature spiritually and psychologically, we become less dependent on hard labor and more dependent upon our own creative nature to succeed. You are part of this evolution. That's why you are alive at this time in history. You were created as an outlet for the Genius, the one Mind of Spirit. This infinitely creative Mind is passing through your mind new ideas every day that can change and transform your life.

Your dreams don't arrive by mistake. They have been hand-delivered to your mind on purpose. They're not sent to torture you or to show you something you *can't* have. Like the trailers you see at the movie theater, your dreams are the coming attractions of your life. They exist as potentialities. Your purpose is to march faithfully toward them.

You are a member of this new creative class. It's time to start using your creative power. The key to discovering your soul's assignment is to listen to and follow the best ideas that flow through your mind. Your future good is tied to your current dreams. Very few people know this and so don't give them much attention. But you know better.

EXERCISE: GENIUS JOURNAL

In the sixteenth century, in his *Journal of Inventions*, Leonardo da Vinci wrote, "I have always felt it is my destiny to build a machine that would allow man to fly." Next to the entry was a sketch for his invention, which he called his flying machine. Clearly he was a man way ahead of his time. And yet because his mind was open to the flow of new ideas from the one Genius Mind, he became known as one of the world's most creative men. Your mind has equal access to the genius that Leonardo da

Vinci had. You are connected to the same Spirit.

Purchase a journal to write or draw in. Keep it handy on your office desk or bedside table to document your best ideas as they emerge.

Create a daily genius session. Sit in quiet contemplation for three ten-minute intervals. Quiet your mind and listen. Allow ideas to emerge naturally. At the end of each session, write down or draw out in your journal whatever comes to mind. Resist self-judgment. Don't try to figure out how the ideas will manifest. Just record them.

You will begin to see a pattern emerge. Make note of it. And then sit in silence again and ask Spirit, "What is the meaning of this pattern? What is next for me to do about these ideas?" Your answer will emerge. When it does, follow the direction you have been given. It will lead to your soul's assignment.

six

Self-Command

Four years ago, I was watching the 2008 Paralympics on television and was introduced to a young man named Marlon Shirley. He was getting ready to run the 100-meter race and defend his prior year's title of gold medal winner. He seemed ready for this defining moment in time. Like all professional athletes, he was accustomed to spending months or even years of hard work preparing for this one big event.

Prior to the race, the station aired a five-minute film on his life, with a heartfelt interview of his adoptive mother. Abandoned at the age of three by his biological mother, who was a prostitute in Las Vegas, Marlon learned to survive with other kids on the street. Eventually, he made his way into the foster care system. But when he was five, a lawn mower accident caused him to lose his left foot.

In the video, his mother talked about the adoption and his troubled youth. She discussed his tenacity and drive to overcome the physical challenges that come from missing a limb. At one point she talked about the emotional challenges an abandoned child faces. She said it was difficult for Marlon to express his feelings and accept love. One day, after being with him, she prayed to God, "I wish my son could just say, I love you." Minutes later, her prayer was answered. He called to say, "Mom, I just wanted to let you know how much I love you." She shed a mother's tear as she recounted the story.

The producers of the piece did an excellent job. By the time the actual race was ready to start, the viewer was deeply invested in him winning. All hopes were on him and the gold medal he would bring home. Even the cameras seemed to be focused on him alone. And more than anything, *I* wanted him to win that race.

As the starter pistol went off, the runners left their mark like a bullet out of a gun. It was all happening so fast, you could hardly take it in. Marlon was in the lead, running ahead of the pack. I yelled out loud to the TV set, "Go, man, go!"

But then something happened. I don't know what; maybe he tripped on the prosthetic or twisted his ankle. Halfway through the race, he fell to the ground with a look of agony on his face as the other runners bolted past him. He was in pain, and tears were pouring out of his eyes as the devastation of the moment began to take effect emotionally. My heart sank as I watched this broken, fallen man lie on the ground in ruins.

He tried to get up, but fell again. He forced himself up again and tried to walk. He was determined to get to the finish line. Paramedics gathered near him to assist, but he refused their help. With tears running down his face, he dragged himself to the finish line! Finally, it was over and I was so emotionally exhausted from watching it, I had to turn the TV set off. I just couldn't accept the defeat.

My thoughts turned to his mother and the devastation she must have felt watching her son fall. I wondered what she would say to him. I wondered how many times she had seen her son fall, and get back up again. I felt sorry for her and for the personal defeat Marlon must have felt.

But then it occurred to me that as an athlete with one foot, he must have triumphed over this kind of thing many times. My pity for him faded as I came to realize he was living the life of his dreams. And like anyone who is in valiant pursuit of a dream, the ups and downs come and go, but the dream lives in the heart forever. I'm sure Marlon will rise again and run another race. You don't keep a man like him down for very long.

Personally, I find Marlon's story very inspiring. To overcome the emotional pain of an abandoned child, only to face the physical challenges of losing a foot must have seemed insurmountable to him. And yet, somehow he did it and went on to become an Olympic athlete. That's remarkable!

Inscribed on the wall in my home office are the words of Robert Browning, "Ah, but a man's reach should exceed his grasp, or what's a heaven for?" Those words serve as a daily reminder to live a full life, to keep reaching for the highest possible good I can imagine. Seeing them each day increases my determination to not accept less than my heart's true desire. Like Marlon Shirley, I would rather fall down on the ground reaching for my dream, than to have never pursued it at all. It's not the end or the finish line that matters. It's the character you build and the life you create on your way.

To fully own yourself, to have a full sense of your worth and power, you must begin by taking command of your life. As long as someone else is running your life and making your decisions, you'll never find your power and be your true, authentic self. Like Marlon, you've got to run your own race no matter how it turns out in the end.

A Frog Boiling in Water

I don't know from personal experience, but I'm told if you have a pot of boiling water on the stove and you drop a frog in it, he'll immediately jump out. But if you put a pot of *cold* water on the stove, then put the frog in it and slowly heat the water, the frog will stay in the pot and eventually be boiled to death. Guess who the frog is? It's you. You're the frog!

Ralph Waldo Emerson wrote, "We but half express ourselves, and are ashamed of that divine idea which each of us represents." We live *half* lives. We're *partly* happy and *somewhat* in love. Sometimes we're awake, but most of the time we're still asleep. A *portion* of us is in the game but we're not fully in yet.

We dream our dreams, but we don't do the follow-up work to make them come true. We ask for our healing, but we don't participate in it. We don't want to change anything about ourselves to get healed. We're not living whole lives. We're *halves,* just trying to get by.

This is by no means a judgment or condemnation. We don't get this way by *conscious* choice. We're slowly simmered, like the frog. Little by little each day, we buy into one asinine idea at a time, one false belief or fearful rant, each one pulling us slowly down into lowered expectations, just slowly enough that we don't notice it, like the frog in the pot.

He's probably thinking, "Wow. This is great. The water is refreshing. How nice of them to give me a spa treatment." But then, before he knows it, he's dead! That's what's happening to you. It happens to all of us before we have time to notice. Slowly the lowered expectations of the fearful masses start to take over our minds and control our thinking. Before long, after watching hundreds of television ads by drug companies, we start experiencing symptoms of disease. And then as time passes and we grow older, we become convinced our best days are all behind us.

Ever so slowly, we start to see fewer and fewer good opportunities in life and more and more obstacles. And all of this happens at such a snail's pace that we don't notice it. Until one day we wake up and we're not happy anymore and we don't know why.

This is the effect of not having command of your life. You become one of the unconscious masses being slowly simmered to death. Before you know it, your whole life has been turned into half.

"I Wished to Live Deliberately"

There is a difference between spirituality and religion. Religion was founded by humanity to heal the sense of separation we sometimes feel from God. At its best, it can provide a clear moral compass for its followers. It can bring comfort to sufferers and hope to the helpless.

At its worst, however, religion can be as Karl Marx suggested: "the opiate of the masses." It can help people rationalize their suffering. It can provide a comfort station for mediocre lives, for those who forego a powerful, dynamic life here and now to wait for some future reward in heaven. It can fuel our self-righteousness by giving us a chance to say, "I'm right. You're wrong! My religion is right and yours is wrong."

By contrast, spirituality is an *arousal*, an awakening. It is a call for the Genius within you to come forth. It affirms power present in the now, ready for you to use. It ignites a Divine spark within you, calling you to a greater life.

Starting with American Transcendentalists like Ralph Waldo Emerson and Henry David Thoreau, religion began to take a turn on this continent. A new way of thinking about our relationship to God started to emerge during the days just prior to the Civil War, when questions began to arise about the souls of men. Iconoclastic as it was for its time, this new movement had its roots in ancient wisdom.

The new spirituality claimed that the highest authority resides within us, not in some external deity that acts as an overlord, nor a government which tries to dictate or legislate morality. By watching what is *naturally* occurring around us, Thoreau claimed we can learn how to live in alignment with Nature, not through the outdated doctrine of what Emerson called "dead institutions." And so Thoreau excused himself from society and went to Walden Pond where he said, "I wished to live deliberately. . . . I wanted to live deep and suck out all the marrow of life." And it was there that he observed what twenty-first-century science holds commonplace, that Nature is intelligent. It is filled with an energy and Presence.

If you put a potted plant near a window, it will naturally bend toward the light, the source of its growth and nourishment. The intelligence inside it instinctively knows to do this. When there's a storm and the thunder starts to crash, my dog, Jack, searches for me in the house and stays very close. His instincts tell him to get close to his protector and the source of his good.

Just as Thoreau suggested, there are lessons to be learned here from Nature. If you're as smart as the plant, you too will lean toward the Light of Spirit. You'll turn to the Source of your good where you can be nourished and grow. And if you're as smart as my dog Jack, when you're scared or uncertain of your future, that's when you'll stay really close to God, which is your protector and supplier of everything good.

But if you try to make it on your own, without any connection to your Source, you will suffer the fate of the masses and be lulled back to sleep with lowered expectations and mediocre lives. The opiate of your religion may comfort your limitations for a while, but like all drugs it will soon wear off and you will be stuck in the same life.

The alarm is ringing. This is your wake-up call. It's time to stop accepting less than what you really want from life. It's time to think bigger and live better. It's time to raise your expectations and place a demand upon the Power that resides within you. It's time for you to do as Thoreau did, to live deliberately and suck out all the marrow out of life.

There is no greater authority than the wisdom inside your own soul. External authority is an oxymoron. No one knows better what is right for your life than you do. Others may suggest or opine. Religion may try to scare you into conforming to its doctrine. The government may attempt to legislate your morality. But all of these external forces will fail. Nothing will bring you peace and satisfaction but your own true authentic nature.

Make your own choices. Set your values. Decide the direction you want to go in and start taking steps. Don't wait for someone else to approve of you or society to value who you are. That may take a lifetime. You are a unique individual designed to take your own journey through life. You're not a dog. Dogs travel in packs. You are meant to forge your own adventurous path.

THREE EXERCISES:
SELF-COMMAND

ONE. You are more than just your body. You are a spirit temporarily housed in a physical body. Just as your body has certain physical needs, so does your spirit. To stay healthy and vibrant, your spirit needs to know and feel its connection to your Source. Pray, meditate or chant daily. Do whatever comes naturally to sense your bond with the Creator.

TWO. Take some time to write down where it is in life you have started to accept less. Be completely honest with yourself. We tend to rationalize our limitations or find excuses for them. Resist this temptation. Resist judging yourself. We're all doing the best we can with what we know. You accepted what you did in the past because that's what you thought was good enough, and now it isn't anymore

THREE. If you could have everything your way, if you could design your own life, what would it look like? What would your relationships be like? What career would you choose? If you absolutely knew you were powerful, how would you carry yourself? How would you speak? How would you treat yourself? How would you treat others?

Start designing the life you want to live. Make a plan for the four areas of a balanced life: health, relationships, finance and career. Create a storyboard for each one that has images and pictures of the life you want to create for yourself. Write affirmations on each one or use headlines from magazine articles that speak what you want to create. Place the storyboard in a location where you can see it each day. It will impress your mind and cause your newly designed life to come into fruition.

What the FIP?

Twentieth-century American philosopher Dr. Ernest Holmes wrote, "The manifest Universe is the result of the self-contemplation of Spirit or God." Imagine an entire universe created just because God was thinking about itself. Trillions of stars, billions of planets, all of time and space infinitely expanding, just because God had a creative idea. It blows my mind to think of Spirit constantly making something new, engaged in an endless act of creation.

Think about it: Every single snowflake that's ever fallen on this planet in its five-billion-year history has had a different design. Out of the seven billion people in our world today, not one of them has the same DNA. Every leaf on every tree is unique. Every flower that ever blooms is an original. Every sunrise, every sunset, is a masterpiece of art. We're surrounded by the Genius humbly displaying itself before us every day, and we're looking at the asphalt! That's like visiting the Louvre in Paris, surrounded by the masterpieces of the world's greatest artists and yet staying in the bathroom staring at the toilet.

I remember my art class in third grade and how my creativity soared back then. Like any kid that age, I couldn't wait to run home and show my parents the masterpiece I created with just my little fingers and some paint. When we're young, we're so in touch with that creative spirit.

Picasso said, "Every child is an artist. The problem is how to remain an artist once he grows up." We get dulled down and dumbed down by the monotonous chores of adult life and forget who we are until we're reminded. It's easy to lose touch with the Power that resides within us and forget that its nature is also our own, that we were designed by our Creator to express our own creative talents.

In 2008, the movie *The Curious Case of Benjamin Button* came out. It was an unusual tale about a child born as an old man who got younger as the years progressed. So instead of getting older like we all do, Benjamin spent his life growing young. And it made me think about how different life would be if we could somehow manage to do that, not physically of course, but spiritually.

If we could keep the wisdom and depth that comes with age and then grow younger in spirit, even though our bodies might be old and wrinkled, our spirit would still be creative and adventurous. And then maybe somehow we could retain our enthusiasm for change.

Think back to the day when you felt most creative, most vibrant. When did you feel the most connected to creativity? Since necessity is often the mother of invention, perhaps it was a time when you didn't have much money.

When is the last time you felt something you've never felt before? What was your last *original* thought? How long has it been since you had a conversation with someone who doesn't support your political or spiritual views without getting mad?

As we get older, it's *comfort* we seek, not originality—and that's the problem. Comfort stifles creativity. We want to wear comfortable clothes and comfortable shoes. We want to eat comfort food. We want to be around people who think like we do because it's more comfortable that way.

Emerson warns that if we "sit on the cushion of advantage," we go to sleep. So something gets lost in our quest for comfort, and it's not just our conscious awareness. We lose our creativity. We lose our ability to change and grow.

Outside your comfort zone, just beyond the recliner and the remote for the TV, lies an invisible field. I call this the FIP—the *field of infinite possibility.* That's where God lives, in the FIP. In the FIP, anything is possible. Everything is just a potentiality waiting to take form. Every new invention, all of our future technologies and masterpieces of art that have yet to be created are in the FIP. Your lover is in there waiting for you. Your highest good and greatest success is in the FIP. The thing you want more than anything else in the whole world lies just inside the field of infinite possibility.

And all that's required of you to get there is to use your creative mind, the same mind God uses to contemplate its nature. Imagine your good and believe in it. Follow your best ideas into the FIP. There's a destiny awaiting you there if you have the courage to think something new.

You do not have to be limited by your past or current conditions. They repeat themselves on a loop because you continue to give them your attention. Withdraw your thought from them. Detach from the emotional hold they have placed on you.

You have been created in the image and likeness of Spirit, therefore empowered with your own creative abilities. Take command of the creative power of your own mind. Start to imagine life the way you really want to live it. See it in your mind's eye. Feel it in your heart. Then release the images, thoughts and feelings into the FIP, that invisible field of infinite possibility that you are submerged in. Like seeds planted in rich, fertile soil, they will begin to take form.

Full Presence of Mind

The dictionary defines *self-command* as "full presence of mind; self-confidence." This is not something you can purchase at a store or order online. Full presence of mind is more than just a conscious thought or two throughout the day. You don't gain self-confidence overnight. It is a process that unfolds over time through commitment and determination.

Most people are unaware that their thoughts are causative. They don't know that what thoughts they choose to entertain in their minds on a regular basis create the quality of their lives. So they just allow any negative drama or fearful thought to gain entrance into their mind. And of course random, uncontrolled thoughts create inconsistent results. This is why most people's experience is: one or two good days, then a bad one, then one or two more good ones and then a horrible week.

Having full presence of mind requires regular and consistent practice. If you were trying to gain expertise in some field of work, you would give regular attention to its study. That same truth applies to gaining access to your mind's creative power. It won't happen with just an occasional effort. It requires daily work.

Don't let this overwhelm you. If you have work to do on self-confidence, just keep plugging along. As cliché as it may be, the journey of a thousand miles really does start with the first step. Without taking that first step, you can never get to your destination. Just stay on track and keep moving.

Become conscious of your thoughts. When your thoughts drift to the future or past, gently bring them back to the present. In conversation with others, give all of your attention to listening. Resist planning what you will say next. If you catch yourself staring at the television set without really enjoying what you're watching, turn it off. Don't numb out on unconscious activity. Stay awake.

Work daily to remove the negative monkey chatter from your mind. Let it have its voice. Don't try to drown it out. Just let it pass through your mind without allowing it to retain space. Affirm: "All is well. I am safe. I am becoming more and more clear each day." In time and through regular practice, you will have full command of your mind and will be able to use it to create the results you want to see in your life.

Make It Go Away

As a young man I was filled with passion and desire. Like many young people, the ideas flowing through my mind were electric. There were so many things I wanted to do and see in the world. I could hardly contain my energy.

As I grew older and became faced with the harsh reality of the workaday world of making a living and paying bills, my enthusiasm began to fade. As I watched my age turn from twenty to thirty in a decade that seemed to pass more quickly than I ever thought possible, I started to lose hope that my dreams would ever come true.

At some point I remember thinking, "I wish they would just go away. I wish I never had this desire to be more." But it was too late. It was already there inside me. My only choices were to follow my dreams or try and squelch them. I knew if I didn't start honoring that desire within me to be more and express more, that my life would end up stinking like rotten meat. And if I continued to ignore those innate desires, at some point there would be some kind of explosion. I don't know whether it would have been physical or emotional. But it surely would have caused a major ruckus.

Your desire to express more won't go away. If you listen to that desire and take action toward it, however, not only will you take command of your life, you'll also see your greatest dreams become manifest.

The Spirit that lives within you is so powerful, if you don't find a way to let it out, if you don't find a way to be yourself and fulfill your innate potential, then what you do not let out will torture and destroy you. And that's not a threat. It's just a statement of truth. It's like the warning label on the package of life.

If you don't find your way to love, your desire for it doesn't just go away. It festers inside of you until one day you wake up bitter and angry that you never found the love your soul aches for. If you don't find what's yours to do in this world, that thing that God made you to do or be in life, you'll be haunted by your dreams instead of compelled by them. They'll serve as a constant reminder of what you never had the courage to do.

We don't die all at once. We die in small portions. Little by little each day, we buy the product the world is desperate to sell us: the mediocre existence that so many people have accepted for themselves and the low expectations that keep them cemented in that life.

Make sure that you honor your dreams. Trying to pretend they don't exist is not a workable strategy. It is a setup for failure. They will not go away. Take one small action toward the best idea in your mind each day. Steady progress and effort will lead you to your best life.

Which Path to Take

In his poem "The Road Not Taken," Robert Frost wrote, "Two roads diverged in a wood, and I, I took the one less traveled by, and that has made all the difference." There are two paths to choose from in life, the one trampled and traveled on by the masses, and the one you must forge on your own. While it's important to study history and be aware of what mistakes have been made in the past, it's equally valuable to know when to boldly step into a future of your own making.

Taking command of your life requires you to step away from the crowd and make your own path. Genius always travels alone. It is not concerned with the approval of others, nor does it need it. To travel this path, you will have to leave behind any need for approval. As comforting as it may be to have the validation of others, it will keep you on the path to average existence.

To fully own yourself, to be in command of your life, you must be a nonconformist. Prepare yourself. The crowd will be greatly displeased if you decide to step off the well-traveled path. Stand ready to be ridiculed. Get used to hearing them shout their fears. They will try to impress you with their doubts. Let the voices of conformity fade into the background. Keep moving. You're on the right path if a growing number of people are annoyed by your courage.

This doesn't mean that you blatantly ignore what others say. Seek wise counsel. Listen to those whom you respect, the ones who've forged their own way in life. A few have gone before you and can measure the distance and point out where the potholes are on the path. Take their advice into consideration, but always trust your own intuition first. The Spirit that lives inside you knows better than those around you. Follow it faithfully. It will project light on the path so you can see ahead into the distance.

Don't be surprised if some of your closest friends and family members withhold their support or approval. They may be your harshest critics. Though their intentions are probably to keep you from disappointment and harm, even they can't see the path your soul directs. Your courage may frighten them. In time, they may come to understand your bold action. However, don't depend on it.

When faced with a choice between paths, go within and ask, "Which one leads to my highest good?" You will receive guidance as to which one to choose. The Intelligence within you knows your destiny and where it lies. It will direct you. One path will become more compelling or a door may open leading you toward it. The choice will become clear if you take time to access your innate wisdom.

Once you receive guidance, take bold steps. Trample the ground in front of you. Burn bridges behind you so you're not tempted to retreat. Put yourself out in front of your dreams so there's no turning back. Insist on your good. There can be no denying it. The Spirit that led you to take the path will not let you down.

Three Potholes on the Path

NUMBER ONE: CONFORMITY

> *For non-conformity the world whips you with its displeasure. To believe your own thought, to believe that what is true for you in your private heart is true for all men,—that is genius.*
>
> —RALPH WALDO EMERSON,
> "Self-Reliance"

You are an individual, specifically created to be unique. You will never be like anyone else, nor will you find happiness in trying to be. Give yourself the freedom of your own expression. Enjoy being yourself. Trying to conform to the needs of others will not bring the promised comfort it advertises.

In time, your choice to conform will make you very uncomfortable. Slowly your soul will die.

NUMBER TWO: CONSISTENCY

> *A foolish consistency is the hobgoblin of little minds,*
> *adored by little statesmen and philosophers. . . . With*
> *consistency a great soul has simply nothing to do.*
>
> —RALPH WALDO EMERSON,
> "Self-Reliance"

Consistency is not a human trait. We are not consistent, nor have we been designed to be by our Creator. We are, by nature, creative and adventurous. God has made us to love. We are artists, lovers and poets. Life is an *art*, not a science. It requires inconsistencies and paradox.

It is okay to say what you know today and then contradict it tomorrow. You are supposed to eclipse each day's knowing with the next. As you grow in your awareness of the Power that resides within you, the need for consistency gives way to wisdom.

NUMBER THREE: UNDERSTANDING

> *Is it so bad, then, to be misunderstood? Pythagoras*
> *was misunderstood, and Socrates, and Jesus, and*

Luther, and Copernicus, and Galileo, and Newton,
and every pure and wise spirit that ever took flesh.
To be great is to be misunderstood.

—RALPH WALDO EMERSON,
"Self-Reliance"

Why is it so important that people understand you? Do you need for people to understand your choices before you can accept them as right? Understanding is not a prerequisite to love. You can love people completely and not understand them at all.

Follow your own path. If it makes sense to *you*, that's enough. You don't have to explain it to others. You have a vision they may not possess. You see things that others may never be able to see. Don't wait for people to understand you before you take action. Be prepared to travel your path alone if necessary.

Take a Stand for Your Worth

In the early 1980s, after searching a long time for the right and perfect job, I was hired as the general manager of a European furniture store. With a large staff to supervise, a great salary and promised trips to Italy each year, I thought to myself, "Hallelujah, Jesus, I've hit the jackpot!"

I'm not the kind of person who needs a lot of supervision,

so I was pleased to learn that the only person I would report to was the owner, John White (not his real name). I'll never forget that man as long as I live. John ended up being quite the tyrant. I called him "little Hitler." He was condescending, abusive and demeaning. And just like many of my past relationships and bosses before him, one day I let him go too far.

After I had been employed for about a month, one afternoon he completely humiliated me in front of several members of my staff on the sales floor. I was so flabbergasted that I just stood there speechless. I went home that night tortured over what to do about it, torn between two voices in my head—one that said, "Set your boundaries and stand up for yourself. Don't let anyone disrespect you like that!" And another that said, "You need this job. You better keep your mouth shut and lie low."

As I lay awake, trying to rationalize the latter voice, saying to myself, "Well, he was probably just having a bad day. He didn't mean it. He won't do it again," I knew I was lying to myself. I knew he was going to be abusive again, because that was his nature. In the short time I had been employed there, I watched him treat several people poorly, even his own mother.

The next morning I prayed for courage and went to work. When I arrived, I called John into my office and said,

"Look, I don't know what happened to you yesterday. Maybe you were just having a bad day. But don't ever disrespect me like that again. I don't disrespect you, so don't do it to me."

Oh, my God, you should have seen the look on his face. He was absolutely dumbfounded. I thought I was going to have to pick the man's jaw up off the floor. I don't think anyone had ever stood up to him before. Everyone was too afraid.

I wish I could say everything changed that day and he never disrespected me again, but that's not true. In the three years I worked for him, I had to have that conversation several times, each time taking a stand for my own worth and value. But it was like a training ground for my character and a practice session for setting healthy boundaries. I learned a lot about who I am in the process. And in time, I got really good at standing up for myself.

Having those crucial conversations with someone who's crossed the line is very difficult, but in the end they will always serve you well. You have to tell people how you want to be treated, what is acceptable behavior and what is not. Until you speak up, they will treat you the same way they treat others.

Never let anyone disrespect you, no matter who they are or what position they hold. Stand up to them, even if on the inside you're trembling. Allowing others to treat you poorly dishonors the presence of Spirit that lives inside of you. It ignores your worth and sets a precedence that others will follow.

SEVEN PRACTICAL STEPS TO BUILDING SELF-WORTH

STEP ONE. Stop praying for anything except an awareness of your value. Pray daily. Support your prayer with a personalized affirmation such as: *Every day I am growing in awareness of my value.*

STEP TWO. Make choices that cause you to feel good about yourself. Make the choice that has long-term benefits, not short-lived pleasure. When you make these choices, pat yourself on the back for choosing them.

STEP THREE. Stop putting yourself down to other people. Stop talking about what you don't like. Stop telling your "story." It is not the most interesting part of your life. Stop identifying with people who suffer. You are not a martyr. If you catch yourself doing this, be gentle. Say to yourself, "That's the old me. That's not who I am anymore."

STEP FOUR. Get in touch with your passion. Get involved in creating your dream life. Follow your best ideas. The road to happiness is paved with love and passion. It's hard to think poorly of yourself when you have a great life. A great life is created by following great ideas. The currency of an Infinite Mind is new ideas. God has given you a plethora of new ideas. Take one and follow it.

STEP FIVE. Exercise daily. People who exercise daily enjoy a greater sense of self-value. Your body was not meant to be stationary. It was designed for movement. Find some kind of physical activity that you enjoy and do it regularly.

STEP SIX. Schedule pleasant events and activities. Meet a friend for lunch. Invite a colleague home for dinner. Take time to be with your family. Plan a vacation. Make art. Rent a movie. Do something fun.

STEP SEVEN. Start treating yourself like someone you love. Be kind when you make mistakes. Forgive yourself quickly and move on. You are doing the best you can with what wisdom you possess.

The Ignorance of Society

When I was in high school in the early 1970s, there were only three different groups of kids. First on the social hierarchy were the *jocks*. They were the athletes, football players, track runners; the *popular* kids. Second were the *stoners*, the hippies who wore their hair long, marched for peace, smoked pot and said things like "Far out, man!" At the bottom of the ladder were the *geeks*, the ones who studied hard, wore big, black plastic-rimmed glasses and huddled together at the same table in the lunchroom, apparently planning their takeover of the world, because that's eventually what they did (i.e., the founders of Google, Facebook, Twitter and a host of others).

This pigeonholing of people into different categories is something society does well. It is very fond of lumping people together into groups and subgroups, and then judging them all accordingly. Society can make some pretty ridiculous generalizations such as: "All Mexicans eat tacos," "African American people can dance" and "All gay men love to decorate."

While I'll admit I do know a number of African Americans who like to dance and a gaggle of gays who can decorate the hell out of an otherwise beige box of a house, somehow I think we're more than just the stereotypical roles we get thrown into by society.

It's true; Nature does create in *patterns*, so there will always be groups of people with certain similarities. But that doesn't mean that's *all* we are. We're more than our social class, gender, ethnicity or sexual orientation. We're more than blue states or red states.

We are individual creations of an infinite Mind, of a God that announces each time it creates: *Behold, I make all things new*. Every individual is a once-in-a-lifetime opportunity for Spirit to be expressed as a never-again-repeated-in-all-time-and-history unique person. So our value as individuals will always eclipse whatever category society tries to cram us into.

The people around you may feel more comfortable by putting you in a box and assessing your worth based on which category you fit into, but be sure you're not doing it, as well. Don't be limited by any pigeonhole society tries to force you into. Don't fall victim to their analysis. If there's going to be a glass ceiling, make sure you're not the one creating it.

I have a friend who grew up in South Africa during the Apartheid system. When he was a young boy in grade school, he asked questions the adults around him weren't comfortable answering such as, "Why do the black children have to sit in the back of the room?"

When he became a young man, he was required by the government to join the South African military. Once when he was in uniform on a train, he saw another young man running to catch the train before it left the station. His instincts said to reach down and help him. But before he could respond, the police stepped in with riot gear and clubs and beat the man half to death just because he had mistakenly tried to enter a car that was for "whites only." My friend stood there in horror and watched helplessly.

You don't have to go too far back in our own history to find that level of ignorance and prejudice. Not that long ago, the Congress of the United States was debating whether black people had souls like white men, or were soulless creatures like farm animals and should be bought and sold as such.

So let's just admit it: Society has been wrong every time when it comes to assessing a woman's worth and a man's value. Society is deaf, dumb, blind and ignorant. It cannot see beyond the thin veneer of superficiality. And that's probably why the great abolitionist and poet Ralph Waldo Emerson wrote, "Society everywhere is in conspiracy against the manhood of every one of its members. . . . Whoso would be a man must be a nonconformist."

To be true to your authentic nature, you must stand on your own, apart from the crowd. Don't yield yourself to the low expectations of society. Don't give them more reason to rank you and file you away in some low grouping. Society will always be anxious to categorize and judge you. So it's up to you to make yourself an exception to the rule, to not conform to their assessment of your character and talent.

What if society has been wrong about you all along? What if you're more than the skin-colored body you carry around every day? What if your social class is irrelevant and what you own doesn't matter? What if your value has nothing to do with what you can accumulate on the *outside* of life, but from what already lives inside of you, in this deep well of personage?

To Infinity and Beyond

Think about where you are right now. What is your physical location? What city or town do you live in? By using your imagination, move out from it as though you are traveling through the air somehow. See the city below you. Now go further. See the state you live in and then country. Continue your travels further into space. Look below to see the Earth in all its magnificence. Now go past it into the galaxy and then beyond.

How far would you have to go to reach the perimeter of the universe? How many trillions of miles or light-years would you travel to reach the end of all time and space? Of course, this isn't possible for many reasons. First of all, there are no known vehicles that can travel such an enormous distance. Second, the universe is expanding so quickly that you could never reach its end.

This exercise of imagination is to help you understand the boundlessness of the universe. It is to give you a perspective on where you fit into the picture. Now consider this equation:

The distance you can travel *outside* your body to the edge of the universe is equal to the depth of what is *inside* your being. Distance outside you = Depth inside you.

This is the microcosm inside the macrocosm, and vice versa. Perhaps this is why Jesus said, "Behold, the kingdom of God is within you" (Luke 17:21). You did not enter life as an empty shell. Your soul has infinite depth. Within you lies an endless capacity to love. You have instant access to an ancient and eternal wisdom. You can wonder about anything and find an answer as you explore the depth of an Infinite Mind.

You're much more than the category society has prodded you into. Your value has nothing to do with your physical body. You have the universe inside of you and its infinite potential. This means you will always be learning something new about your capacities. You will always have some nuance to discover in your character and the personalized way you experience life. And even when your body dies, your soul will live on forever.

seven

The Final Frontier

According to a recent National Geographic Channel study, at least eighty million Americans believe that UFOs exist. Other polls record as much as 80 percent of the country believing that intelligent life exists somewhere other than Earth. And certainly the odds would be in their favor.

There are approximately three hundred sextillion stars in the universe. That's a three followed by twenty-three zeros. Or to make it more personal, there are about fifty trillion cells in your body. If you multiply that by six billion people, you get the number of stars in the known universe. Rotating around those stars are billions upon billions of planets, some of which can sustain life as it is on Earth. Chances are, in a universe with three hundred sextillion stars and billions of planets, life exists somewhere other than our world.

People often ask me, "Dr. Chris, do you believe there's intelligent life somewhere other than Earth?" And I always say, "I'm not even sure there's intelligent life *here!*" With all of our petty bickering, useless wars and arguments over who has the right god, I'm not sure we exhibit that much intelligence ourselves.

I know people who claim to have seen a UFO and they ponder, "I wonder why they don't land and show themselves." Well, that's one question I'm pretty sure I know the answer to. My friend Stephanie and her husband, Rick, were invited to a dinner party at another couple's house. When they arrived at the doorstep and were about to knock on the door, they could hear the other couple inside fighting like cats and dogs. Rather than involve themselves in their squabble, they just turned around and went home. Maybe that same thing happened to the extraterrestrials who checked us out. They probably said, "Oh, hell no! Let's come back in a thousand years or so. Maybe they'll be more advanced by then."

I've always been a big science fiction fan. I was a typical adventurous twelve-year-old boy in 1969 when everyone in America gathered around their TV sets to watch Neil

Armstrong step foot on the moon. When I was a young boy, I used to run home from school to watch *Star Trek*. "To seek out new life and new civilizations, to boldly go where no man has gone before," that was my fantasy. If it were possible to travel out into space and be on a mission to discover new worlds, I'd be the first to sign up. Can you imagine how cool that would be?

There's something within the human spirit that has us seek. We want to know what's out there among the stars. We want to find out if we're alone. That adventurous spirit is what drove Christopher Columbus west and what calls us out into space. It's as if the Universe itself is calling us out, saying, "Come see what I've created."

But maybe we've misunderstood this call. Perhaps it's not so much a call to explore outer space as it is to explore *inner* space. Perhaps the new world we seek out there has been *within* us all along.

The problem is, we're so outwardly focused. Nothing in our culture says go within, so we tend to think the solution to our problems lies out there somewhere in the world. We even put God out there just beyond the sky, watching us from a distance. So, when we get into trouble and think of what needs to be done to solve our problems, it never occurs to us to look within. The first thing we do is take action externally. We hire an attorney, get a better job, take a pill or find someone to date. Everything tends toward outer solutions. So it's no wonder we'd be fascinated with discovering new worlds, out there in space.

The solution to our problems individually and also collectively is to discover a new world *within*; to seek out new life and boldly go where we've never gone before. It is to delve the depths of our own consciousness. The call from the Universe isn't to build a spaceship and explore the stars. It's to go within and see what Spirit has placed inside us. It's to find our wisdom and use our own power. The calling is to probe the depths of love and compassion.

Never before in human history has this been so tied to our survival as a species. Although it may appear on the outside that the challenges of our time are political and social, the real challenge of the twenty-first century is to discover our spirituality. Dr. Martin Luther King Jr. said, "Our scientific power has outrun our spiritual power. We have guided missiles and misguided men." Perhaps the final frontier isn't somewhere out there among the stars. Perhaps it's much closer than we think.

In 1955, husband and wife songwriters Sy Miller and Jill Jackson wrote a song about their dreams of peace for our world. They believed each of us holds some personal responsibility in this undertaking. They first introduced the lyrics at a weeklong retreat for teenagers who had been purposefully chosen to attend from various religious, ethnic, cultural and social backgrounds. Sy Miller wrote in his own words what happened next: "One summer evening in 1955, a group of 180 teenagers of all races and religions, meeting at a workshop high in the California mountains locked arms, formed a circle and sang a song of peace. They felt that singing the song, with its simple basic sentiment— 'Let there be peace on earth and let it begin with me'— helped to create a climate for world peace and understanding."

During the Christmas holiday season, people pray to God *up there* to send peace *down here* to earth, as if there was some magic wand God could wave that would bring peace to all humanity. It seems to me, at some point we're going to have to grow up as a race and stop looking for someone to come along and rescue us from ourselves. That's a victim's fantasy. Victims sit and hope someone will save them. But that's not what God created us to be. We are not victims. We're powerful co-creators, responsible for our own choices and their consequences.

We've been created as individuals and set free to discover ourselves. And that means we have to evolve individually, one at a time. So peace has to come to your mind first before it can ever be given to those around you. We have to find that peaceful place within our own hearts and then bring it to the world. That's the only way the world can become a more peaceful place. The spiritual journey is an *inward* one, not an outward search for someone to save you from your poor choices.

Go within. Discover the world of possibilities that resides within you. Tap into the infinite depth of love and compassion that resides there and then give it to others. That's how the world will change, not by begging a distant deity for peace, but by letting out the joy and peace that Spirit has placed inside of your own heart.

Gods with Anuses

In 1977, in Woody Allen's movie *Annie Hall*, he hands her a book and says something like, "You need to read this so you can understand where I'm coming from." The book is by Pulitzer Prize–winning author Ernest Becker called *The Denial of Death*. In it Mr. Becker writes, "We are gods with anuses."

This is our dilemma: We are immortal beings in mortal bodies, spiritual beings connected to eternity encased in these heart-pumping, breath-gasping animal bodies. We are inlets and outlets for the Divine, mortal, skin-encapsulated bags of water with an eternal spirit: gods with anuses.

When I was a young boy, I had so much energy that I

would literally go outside and just run around in circles. I sure wish I had that energy today. I would use it for more productive things. When we come into life in fresh bodies, we feel the rush of youth. Our energy is high. We have full ownership of our spirit. We've just arrived from the heavens, so we feel cocky and immortal. There's nothing we can't do, no dream too big, no mountain too high to climb. We are gods!

Youth is about learning the limits of our strength, finding the perimeter of our influence. It's the time where we ask serious life questions such as: How many days and nights can I stay awake partying before I pass out? How fast can I drive a car before it falls apart? How much can I drink before I puke?

In youth, we're trying to find the limits, testing ourselves to see how far our bodies can be pushed and how much they can endure. And it doesn't take long to find those limits. If we don't find them on our own, *time* will show us. What the body can do at twenty, it can't do at fifty, at least not for as long.

Slowly we begin to realize we might be more mortal than we think and the time we have here is passing more quickly than ever. Human life has a way of bringing you face-to-face with the cold reality of your physical limitations.

And time has a way of not only shrinking our bodies but

also our expectations. It convinces us to lower our standards. As we grow older, it becomes easy to lose our way and forget our Divine lineage. We forget we're essentially dreamers sent from the stars to make our dreams come true, to bring heaven to earth. Living in the dirt for too long convinces you that you *belong* there and so after a while you just stop looking up at the stars.

In 1508, Michelangelo began painting the ceiling of the Sistine Chapel. It would take him four years to complete. In his fresco, he depicted the greatest desire known to man: to touch the hand of God, to recapture our Divinity. Our greatest desire is to stretch beyond our humanity, to get our feet out of this stinking mud and regain our status as gods.

It would take almost five hundred years after Michelangelo painted his fresco before we could start to make his vision come true. The same year the movie *Annie Hall* came out, in 1977, we reached again for the heavens but this time for real, not just in a painting. *Voyager I* was launched that year.

Just in case you haven't been following the progress of our first space probe, it is currently eleven billion miles from the star we call the Sun, traveling out into the universe looking for answers. *Voyager I* will be the first man-made object to ever leave our solar system.

We will not be stopped by gravity. With an infinite universe to explore, we will not be confined as prisoners to one planet. And we will not have our spirits confined to bodies either. We have much more inside us to be let out.

You're more than your body or whatever limits it may have. You're more than your problems, struggles and conditions. You're more than your physical or financial assets. You are a Light-being, a spiritual entity, a Divine appointment. What you have within you comes from heaven itself.

In his popular poem *Pass On*, my friend Michael Lee wrote, "Death does not come when a body is too exhausted to live. Death comes, because the brilliance inside us can only be contained for so long." The Occupier, the Spirit within our bodies, can't be confined to a physical form for very long. It's just too limiting. When our work is done here, our spirit has to rejoin others who've gone before us.

If you think this idea that we're gods seems a bit high and mighty, consider this before you pass judgment: In Emerson's essay "The Oversoul," he wrote, "From within or from behind, a light shines through us upon things, and makes us aware that we are nothing, but the light is all." There is no *plural* when it comes to God. There's only one God, one Light. Without that Light shining through us, we're nothing but empty shells.

If you've ever been to a funeral and seen an open casket,

you know this is true. When you gaze upon the deceased, it's obvious there's no life in the body. The Spirit that occupied it is gone. And yet people often say the queerest things when faced with this uncomfortable situation. They say, "Oh, she looked so natural." And I always want to reply, "No, she didn't. She looked dead!"

The truth is: Your body can't maintain itself, no matter what you do. The Spirit that lives in it beats your heart and circulates your blood. Without that Divine Intelligence directing every cell in it, your body doesn't exist. So you are part human and part God, part mortal and part immortal. You are a Light-reflector. You are a perfect spiritual being having an imperfect experience. You're a god with an anus.

A Mash-Up of Human and Divine

In some way or another, every faith and philosophy was founded to help us answer the perennial questions of life such as, "Who created us?" "Why are we here?" "What is the meaning of our lives?" All religion, science and art seek to answer those questions. There's something within our spirit that knows we are more than we appear to be, and so we go in search of our true identity.

Jesus advised us not to judge by appearances alone. He knew that what resided in him also resides in us, that some part of who we are is connected to eternity. Philosopher Dr. Ernest Holmes wrote, "We are immortal beings on the pathway of an endless destiny." Though our bodies may be confined to one space in one time, our spirit is limitless. The Life that resides within us will outlive our mortal bodies. It is a traveler through time and space, gathering experience and adventure. So we are some kind of mash-up of human and Divine.

The thing you call yourself is not really you. You are not the image that reflects in the mirror. Your true identity is in Spirit, not body. You are a link in a chain of causation that stretches before and after your life for thousands of generations. How you choose to live your life matters, not only to the people around you, but also to future generations.

Because we are all connected to each other in one great big web of life, every time you choose love over hatred, that choice affects us all. Every time you stop and think *before* you react, each time you show compassion instead of judgment, you're up there on the ceiling of the Sistine Chapel reaching just beyond your grasp to touch the hand of God.

Every time you work to learn and apply spiritual principles to your life, when you push your consciousness to dream something that's just a little bit beyond your reach, you're just like *Voyager I* covering new territory, reaching out into the unknown. And if you keep doing this, one day your small, petty human self will give way. It will reach its own level by its own weight and sink to the bottom, and your Divine self will rise to reach the surface.

Human life is a soap opera of self-created dramas, each one designed to reveal your Divine nature. The stories of your life, both the big dramatic ones and the small unimportant ones, share something in common: They are there to show you who you are. You learn how much courage you have by facing your fears. You learn the limits of love, and how useless it is unless it's balanced with wisdom, each time you survive a ruined relationship. You learn your value and worth by meeting others who question it. Every story of your life has been personally crafted to reveal your Divine nature.

Be careful not to be too drawn into the story. You are more than just a character in a drama. You're the story *writer*. You're the actor on the stage and director of your own drama.

Take a fresh look at your life and see it for what it really is. Instead of just a low-life human struggling to reach Divinity, you are a timeless spirit on an endless journey of love. Keep reaching for the stars. Hold your head up when you walk into a room. When you enter, God enters. Respect the sacred and holy life you carry with you into each new day.

The Top Five

One of my favorite TV personalities is Katie Couric. I've followed her career since she was on the *Today* show in the 1990s. I love her authenticity. She's got one of those happy-cheerleader personalities that a lot of people try to fake, but for her it just seems to come naturally.

Like all of us, Katie's had her share of ups and downs, both in her personal life and in her career. Her husband died of colon cancer at forty-two years old, leaving her with two small children to raise on her own. After she was a huge hit on the *Today* show on NBC, she got tagged to do the *CBS Evening News*, which didn't go well.

Katie's career started in the early 1980s as an assistant assignment editor for CNN in Washington, D.C. That's when she got her first big break. The Washington bureau chief approached her one day and asked her to go to the White House and report on the president's schedule. Needless to say, she was thrilled. She'd never done a TV report before, and to have your first assignment be the White House was quite a coup.

Katie went home from work that night and spent most of the evening talking to a hairbrush, rehearsing for the next day. The next morning, when she went on the air she recited the president's schedule word for word off the AP wire in that singsong voice of hers. When her piece was over, she said she felt more relieved than anything else. By the time she got back to the office, her boss had gotten a call from the president of CNN, whose message was blunt, "I never want to see that girl on the air again!"

When you're out there in the world living from your best ideas and your greatest dreams, inevitably somebody's going to tell you it can't be done. Someone is going to have a negative opinion about every choice you make.

This is what Katie Couric has to say about those people: "Along the way, you're bound to encounter a few naysayers and buzz killers. Maybe they're insecure, maybe they're bitter, maybe they simply lack imagination. Those people need to be strained from your life like sand from a colander of freshly washed seashells."

Your life is created and mostly lived from the five people who are closest to you. They're your inner circle. They match your consciousness. They mirror your beliefs. They parrot your thoughts. And they either bring most of the joy to your life or most of the drama.

Stop and think about those five people. Who are they? Who stands the closest to you? Who do you spend the most time with? Who are you listening to and what are they saying? And more important, what do they want for you? Do they want you to have what *you* want out of life, or are they trying to project their own fears onto your experience? When you succeed at something, do they say, "I knew you could do it. I'm so proud of you"? And when you fail, do they say, "I got your back. Don't worry about this. I'm going to be here for you"?

When I first came to understand spirituality and realized that a whole new world of opportunities was available to me, a flood of new ideas started rushing through my mind. Something really magical happens when you finally get it that the Universe is for you and there's nothing operating against you in life.

When that happened, I'd wake up in the middle of the night with scripts to movies, new ideas for businesses, formulas and equations all spinning around in my head. At first I was confused as to why I was getting all of this information. Now I realize I was touching the Mind of God. I was opening my mind to the Infinite Mind, and a floodgate of creativity started pouring in. As it did, I started sharing all of these new creative ideas with my own inner circle of five friends. I was really excited about them and gushing with enthusiasm.

Much to my dismay, they were not received well. They said, "Now, Chris. You can't do that. You know you're not going to write a movie script. You don't have any money to start a business like that. Who are you kidding?"

It felt like someone had let the wind out of my sails. Every time I would reach for the stars, they would just drag me back down in the dirt. So I started to take an honest look at their lives and realized they were just naysayers and buzz killers, like Katie had described. I asked myself, "Who are these people and how did they get into my life?" I didn't realize at the time that it was my own consciousness that attracted them.

It became clear I needed to strain those people out of my life like sand in a colander. And it wasn't as difficult a task as I imagined. It just happened naturally. There wasn't any big confrontation. We didn't have an argument or anything. I just became more interested in my dreams and what I could do to start living them, while they were interested in repeating and regurgitating their own misery. So we just lost interest in each other, and one day I turned around and they were gone.

I learned something from them, though. I learned your top five ought to be the Fab Five. The people closest to you ought to be your biggest supporters. They should love you unconditionally and be willing to fight for you if they have to. And you need to give to them first the support you ask in return. You need to be one of their Fab Five.

Who are the five people in your life and how are they shaping your choices? What voice do they support—the voice of fear or the voice of faith? Do they lift you up or try to drag you down? Do they love and accept you unconditionally, or are they judgmental and condescending? Take a look around. It might be time to do some straining.

Don't Look Too Closely

I don't like those magnifying mirrors that some women use to put on makeup. There's one adhered to the bathroom wall in my vacation home, placed there by the previous owner, but I never use it. It's just too harsh. A female friend of mine said, "After a woman reaches a certain age, she needs some distance, proper lighting and lots of fabric!"

When I take friends to visit New York City who've never been there before, my first stop on the tour is the top of the Empire State Building. Seen from above, New York is an amazing city. I refer to it as "chaos within control." But when you go down the elevator and out into the streets, you can smell urine. And when you spend a day walking the streets of New York, a dirty film covers your body, one that millions of people have left behind as they tramped the streets.

Up close, the world is dirty, crazy and noisy. It is filled with human suffering and struggle. There are strict borders and clear lines of delineation between the haves and have-nots. But when you see that peaceful blue planet from the proper distance of space, you sense the majesty of it being held there gently by some great Power.

When we look at life too closely, we tend to judge too quickly. Stand back a bit and you'll see the full picture. That's the proper perspective for your personal life as well. Don't look too closely. Put some distance between yourself and your experience. The things that happen to you are necessary for the advancement of your soul. Even the things you curse and wish would go away are part of a bigger plan to bring you closer to the Power that resides within you.

Collectively that's what's happening in the world today. We're just starting to awaken to the power and potential that's been left within us by Nature. The rebellions in the Middle East and in other places around the globe reflect this awakening. New generations are taking to the streets demanding their freedom, standing up for their rights to equal opportunity.

We've been carrying this torch in the western world for more than two centuries now, but the word is spreading and the world is waking up. It's a fascinating time to be alive on this twenty-first-century earth! We have a bird's-eye view on global transformation.

What will happen when China awakens, when billions of people rise up to demand liberty and freedom of expression?

It won't be long before the continent of Africa awakens too. And when it does, we'll have come full circle, back to the birthplace of the human race where the seed of consciousness was planted.

It's time to get off our knees and stop worshiping distant deities. It's time to stand up and assume power. We must set aside our petty arguments about religion and honor all paths to God and the sacredness of every life.

Stand back a bit and you will see the bigger picture of what's happening in our world. The continents are awakening. The people are rising up, first in the west, then the Middle East, Europe, Asia and Africa. We grow conscious. It's all part of the Divine plan to bring us to the place where we know ourselves as one people on one planet with one voice saying: "We are here Creator. We are conscious, awake, and ready."

Two Steps Forward and Three Steps Back

On January 20, 1961, newly elected President John F. Kennedy was giving his inaugural address on the steps of the Capitol building in Washington, D.C., anxious and ready to take the helm of the nation. He said, "Let the word go forth from this time and place . . . that the torch has been passed to a new generation." Nearly three years later, I would come home from school to find my mother crying, staring at the TV in shock. The president had been shot. Who would do such a thing? How could this happen? Five years later, Dr. Martin Luther King Jr. would suffer the same fate.

Historically speaking, when someone steps away from the crowd to lead us with a clear vision of our greatness, we kill them. We fear our genius. We doubt our innate abilities. So to silence the message, we kill the messenger. President Kennedy's voice was silenced that fateful day in November 1963 by an assassin's bullet and Dr. King's in April 1968, but not their vision for the country they loved. Their dreams are still alive in our hearts as we work to manifest them.

I get frustrated sometimes watching the snail's pace at which the human race evolves. It's hardly visible from the span of one human life. I'm impatient. Sometimes I get discouraged and think, "When are people going to get it? Why is it so hard to see there's no need to fear our differences?" How is that in the twenty-first century gay people have to fight for basic human rights? Why are women still paid less than men? How can we rationalize discriminating against others whose skin pigmentation is different from our own? We try to move forward from our highest ideals, but then seem to get pushed back by our own prejudices and self-destructive behaviors. It's like we're taking two steps forward and three steps back.

My frustration reminds me that once again I am looking too closely and judging too quickly. There's a process unfolding, a Divine plan being played out in the proper sequence. Everything's being transformed from the inside, out. Each of us is on our own path, each of us with our own unique challenges to face and stories to unfold. And yet, somehow, our stories are all intermingled. We're all part of a bigger story, the story of an awakening consciousness for planet Earth. When I can see things from that perspective, it helps me be more patient with myself and more compassionate with others.

We don't collectively arrive all at once, conscious and awake, all seven billion people. We awaken *individually*, as we have been created. And we have to do that one day at a time, one minute at a time, one choice at a time. Don't think you're in this struggle alone. You're not. We're all here together, working out our own issues in our own time. We're growing. We're learning. We're healing.

Things are changing and getting better, even though at times it may appear like you're making no progress at all. Every day brings you a new opportunity to make a new choice, and in so doing, set a new course for your life. Never underestimate the value of the spiritual work you are doing.

It has a cumulative effect on your consciousness and belief system. Stay on course. Keep moving in the direction of your best ideas. If we've learned anything from history, we know that one person with a dream can change everything.

A Trip to Bali

Last year I decided to take a trip to the exotic island of Bali. It was a personal pilgrimage to experience the holiness and sacredness of the Divine. I wanted to set foot on soil of an ancient culture whose spiritual life isn't separate and segregated to just one hour on a Sunday morning. I wanted to know what the Balinese know and feel what they feel.

We've each been fashioned by our Creator with a unique line of communication. Some people feel things. Others see. My connection with Spirit has always been to hear it. I hear its voice. I don't hear conflicting voices in my head telling me to do strange things. I'm not schizophrenic. I just hear one voice, one clear, pure, distinct voice. And I've trained myself to listen to that voice because it's *always* right.

One morning in Bali, I woke up and heard God say something it has never said to me before. Spirit said, "I have a gift for you." And I was thinking, "Cool. I like gifts. Now what could it be? Is it wealth or some kind of healing? Maybe it's something better than that. Maybe my biggest dream is

about to come true, the dream my ego wants to manifest."
As I was thinking to myself about what I wanted, I heard
Spirit say, "You don't decide the gift. I do!"

I spent that day touring the island looking for the gift. I
was like a kid on a treasure hunt searching everywhere. God
said, "I have a gift for you," and by God, I was determined
to find it. On my schedule was a visit to one of Bali's most
sacred sites, a Hindu temple built over a thousand years ago
at the entrance to a cave.

When unusual events take place in a particular location,
or something happens out of the ordinary, it's taken in
Hindu culture to mean that God is present, so a temple is
built on the site. In this case, the cave is filled with bats,
thousands of black bats hanging upside down at the entrance.

The bats don't appear to ever leave the cave, and it runs so
deep into the mountain that it's unknown where it ends.
That's what makes it a mystery. They have no known means
of nourishment. They just hang there all day and night. So
an altar was built a thousand years ago, and then a temple
surrounding it. The bat cave is one of Bali's many holy sites
where people come to pray.

The group I was with was granted special entrance, but
first we had to purchase the appropriate attire. A sarong and

sash are required clothing for all men to enter the temple. Unlike most westerners, our group was scheduled to receive a blessing from the temple priest.

To receive the temple blessing, you must sit on the ground with legs folded and head bowed before the altar. Once you're in the required posture, the Hindu priest stands over you splashing holy water on your face and on top of your head, as you humbly make your offering with hands folded in prayer position. Flowers are given out for the ceremony, and once the priest blesses you with holy water, you are to place them on top of your head. Needless to say, it's a very humbling experience.

So there I am in my crisply starched white shirt sitting on the ground in the dirt outside the entrance of a cave. My face is dripping wet with water. My hair's a mess, my feet are dirty, I'm wearing a sarong, which is basically a woman's skirt. I've got a bunch of flowers sitting on the top of my head. And if that's not enough indignity, for the final part of the ceremony the priest gives you a clump of rice which you're supposed to stick on your forehead right between your eyes.

Just when I thought it couldn't get any more strange or uncomfortable, I look up to see the bats hanging against the cave wall start moving and shaking their wings. I looked around to see what was causing the commotion. To my dismay, there were dozens of huge rats coming out of the cave entrance crawling over the top of the altar!

Now I'm a Virgo, and Virgos don't clean things, we *sterilize* them. We're clean freaks. So, seeing those filthy rats at the altar of this supposedly holy and sacred place totally grossed me out! It was all I could do to not jump up, pull up my skirt, scream like a girl and run. Somehow I kept my composure, finished the ceremony and then hightailed it out of there.

Once outside the gates of the Hindu temple, I heard Spirit's voice say, "That was your gift." And in my mind I was thinking, "Seriously, that's my gift! Are you kidding me? To be put on the ground in the dirt, looking like an idiot and totally grossed out. That's not exactly what I consider a gift."

I spent the next few days trying to figure it all out. How can that be my gift from God? What does it mean? Finally it came to me. My gift from God at the temple in Bali is something Buddhists call *"samma ditthi." Samma ditthi* is the first step on the Noble Eightfold Path to enlightenment, which loosely translated means "right view."

Right view is at the beginning and ending of the path. It simply means to see and understand things as they really are, not as they appear. It means having the right perspective and view of life and all the events and circumstances that make it up. Right view allows you to take in everything, to let it all be what it is, without taking it personally. Right view lets you see things as God sees them, from the point of higher knowing.

Generally in life when something happens to us, we're quick to attach a label to it. It was either good or bad, right or wrong, nice or nasty. Somebody we love dies. We get laid off from a job. We wreck the car and then lament, "Woe is me. How could this happen? Why is God punishing me?"

If something happens we like, such as a promotion at work, a date with someone promising or an increase in income, we say, "I'm blessed. Surely God must be pleased with me." But the truth is, neither one of those is correct. God doesn't bless or curse. It simply is! It gives itself and all it has to everyone equally.

The good in your life today reflects your consciousness, your willingness to believe in and attract it. God hasn't pulled you out of the crowd and said, "To you I will give more." You've pulled yourself out of the crowd of mediocre acceptance. You've lifted yourself above the law of averages that dictates an average experience to the unconscious masses. God doesn't damn either. It doesn't curse some and bless others. It gives. Its Presence is holy and all of its creation is sacred.

That's the gift of right view, the gift I received at the bat cave temple. It's something the Hindus have always taught and known: the truth that *everything* is sacred. On the ground in the filth, with rats crawling around and bat crap dripping down the temple altar, people sit in the midst of it all for a holy blessing!

And if you think about it, that's a pretty accurate account of your life as well. In the midst of all the crap that happens to you, the horrible things, the hardship and troubles you encounter, God is still there. The ground is still holy and the Power to overcome it all is present within you.

Right view—that's the first step on the path of enlightenment, to be able to see through the crap and still claim your good. It means to go through the stuff you don't like and still know that as long as God is present, in the end everything will work out. You'll make it through it. And when you do, an even greater good is waiting for you on the other side.

afterword

With a greater understanding of the Power that resides within and the wisdom of your soul's assignment, it's time to move ahead in life. You are awake, conscious and ready to assume the position Nature intended, that of conscious co-creator. It's time to start using the power of your mind in a constructive manner. Direct your thoughts toward positive means. Give attention to your best ideas. They lead to dreams fulfilled.

Having less than what your heart longs for is no longer acceptable. Charge forward in bold pursuit of your vision. You have a purpose to fulfill and a dream to make come true. The talent you've been given by your Creator is the call. Follow it. It will lead to your destiny.

Step away from the crowd. Be a nonconformist. Trust your gut instincts. They are your connection to the Divine. Don't be hurt by the friends and family members who cannot understand you. What they can't see in themselves, they won't be able to see in you. Their fears are just a way to show concern. Hear them with compassion, but don't let them stop you from moving in the direction of your dream.

You are an uncommon creation, an exclusive and unique expression of Life. There will never be another one like you. You have been designed by Spirit for more than just the mundane tasks of human life.

There is no virtue in suffering. Be sure that you have removed from your mind any belief in its necessity. The unconditionally loving and perfect Mind that created you has no plan for your misery. Its intention for your life is always the fullest expression of who you are.

There's a better way for you to live and a greater purpose to manifest. Don't be lulled back to sleep by the low expectation of the masses. Stay awake!